T0230697

CLOCKWORK
GAME DESIGN

CLOCKWORK
GAME DESIGN

KEITH BURGUN

 Routledge
Taylor & Francis Group
New York London

First published 2015 by Focal Press

711 Third Avenue, New York, NY 10017, USA
2 Park Square, Milton Park, Abingdon, Oxon OX14 4RN

Routledge is an imprint of the Taylor & Francis Group, an informa business

First issued in hardback 2017

Library of Congress Cataloging in Publication Data
Burgun, Keith.
    Clockwork game design / Keith Burgun.
        pages cm
    1. Computer games—Design. 2. Video games—Design.
    3. Computer games—Programming. I. Title.
    QA76.76.C672B859 2015
    794.8'1526—dc23   2014041373

ISBN: 978-1-138-79873-1 (pbk)
ISBN: 978-1-138-42822-5 (hbk)

Typeset in Berling and Futura
By Keystroke, Station Road, Codsall, Wolverhampton

CONTENTS

PREFACE

ELEGANCE

Like many words in the English language, the word *elegance* has a few different meanings. One meaning that's likely to get usage is "beauty": "she wore an *elegant* dress," for example—an entirely positive association.

"Beauty" usually means something like "aesthetically pleasing." But the subjectivity of whether "beauty" should refer to any given thing means that this word is also ineffectual; a person can't be wrong about beauty, at least when it comes to what they personally consider "beautiful." While it feels warm and romantic, the word doesn't actually do much of what words usually do, which is to *describe* something. In the context of a technical textbook, words can be judged by their explanatory power, and, by this metric, "beauty" does not fare well. When a person says that they find something beautiful, all you can glean from this is that they value that thing in some way.

A more useful definition for the term "elegance" might be something like "efficiency"—accomplishing as much as possible with as little as possible. When looked at in this way, elegance is much more well-defined, and it's even possible to loosely quantify. In this case, however, we have almost the opposite problem: people see "efficiency" as a cold, inhuman, or "non-artistic" quality that is best pursued by machines.

Worse yet is the common mistake of believing that achieving efficiency is *easy*. The thinking goes something like this: to be efficient, all you've got to do is plug a few numbers into an algorithm, and you've now got the correct, ideal answer for how to accomplish your task. It's so simple, a primitive computer could do it! The real difficulties, the mythology tells us, are in achieving the "human" or "emotional" things—making people laugh, deep philosophical insight, portraying personality, and the like.

The problem with this way of thinking, at least with regards to game design or any other creative craft, is that in practice there is never some simple algorithm that you can plug numbers into. Game designers operate in an extremely complex world, creating complex machines for complex humans to interact with. In such a context, finding efficiency is every bit as hard as any other task a person can take on, and requires all of the same human/artistic skills of creating a great painting or composing a great piece of music. Art is a mechanical process of problem-solving; an engineering problem and, as such, efficiency is a requirement.

It would be wonderful if we could allow some of that romance we associate with "beauty" to bleed over into our understanding of what "efficiency" is. Perhaps a better use of the term "beautiful" would be to use it to indicate when something is worthy of the same sort of profound positive association that the word "beauty" itself gets. "Beauty" is like glitter that you dust across the surface of other concepts that communicates, "I challenge you to see *this thing* as profoundly positive."

Efficiency is beautiful. But more than that, it's just what we do. Human beings, living in a world of finite resources, must always strive to take the most conservative action. We cannot afford to take five years doing a job that we could achieve in four. All else being equal, we will always choose the option that gets the biggest yield for the smallest investment. In fact, the opposite of efficiency is pure wastefulness, ignorance, or carelessness—all profoundly negative qualities.

Writing, like game design or any other craft, is a constant search for efficiency. We are always placing a stroke, a note, a line, a rule, and then trying to find alternatives that are *more efficient*. In this book, I will generally use the word "elegance" to refer to "efficiency." "Elegance" contains much of the technical definition of "efficiency," along with some of the profound goodness of "beauty." In this way, the word "elegance" itself is *more elegant* than its alternatives.

This book is about the search for elegance in game design.

WHAT IS THIS BOOK?

This book is a guide to better strategy game design. It uses a combination of core philosophy, analysis of existing systems, exercises, critical questions, charts, and other elements to build a consistent and solid process for designing great games.

Something to know up front is that this is *not* a book about game development. This book will not teach you how to manage a team, set deadlines, become a programmer, rig 3D models, or any such technical game development skills.

This book also doesn't spend much time dealing with the practicalities of game design in real life. Whether you've got a $10 million budget and a thousand employees, or whether it's just you designing a game on paper before you go to bed, the principles of good game design apply, and that's what this book focuses on. It's up to you to figure out how best to apply these principles in your own unique situation.

Since this is a book for game designers or people who teach game design, this book assumes that the reader has a basic knowledge about at least some of the most popular games. It assumes that the reader knows things such as the rules to chess, *Tetris*, and *Super Mario Bros*. It does not, however, assume that the reader is an expert on games, so more obscure references will be explained in enough detail to be useful.

STRUCTURE

The first chapter, **Theory**, serves as a basic conceptual and theoretical overview: what is a game? We'll dive deep into the question and get some solid understanding of this form and its values. Also: what other kinds of interactive forms exist, aside from games? How do these relate to, and interact with, strategy games? In this chapter we'll also review some of what has already been said on the topic.

The second chapter, **Anatomy**, is where we really dive into the concept of strategy games. What's the purpose of strategy games? How are strategy games structured—what are their parts, and how do we refer to them? Goals will be discussed in depth. This is also the chapter where many formal definitions will be given.

The third chapter, **Construction**, focuses on the actual application. Here's where we get into the process of actually designing a game. How should we start? Should we start with a thematic idea first and then build from there? At what point should we figure out what the goal of our game is? How do we balance our game? We'll take a look at some good methods for interpreting, processing, and implementing player feedback, one of the most important aspects of designing a game.

The final chapter, **Pitfalls**, looks into some common problems of game design. These are things that you should be aware of and look out for in your own designs.

CHAPTER 1

THEORY

Section 1 GAMES

GAME DESIGN SPECIALIZATION

Relatively speaking, game design is a new discipline. While there have been professional composers, painters, writers, and architects for at least half a millennium, there has only been a class of specialized "game designers" for the past 50 years, and that class has only reached a healthy size in the last 20–25 years or so.

We are still in the early history—or possibly pre-history—of the discipline of game design. If you observe the progression of the discipline of, say, music composition throughout history, you can clearly see that there is a massive increase in the quality of work around the time that an institutional study and respect for the craft began. Much of our understanding of music composition is due to the act of Renaissance churches actually hiring people to compose music. While there had always been "people who composed music" before that, with this decision a class of music-composers was created. These were people who specialized in music composition, whose job it was to compose great music. When it's your full-time job to make the best music you can, that means you have time to start asking serious questions about your craft, and that's how progress happens.

With the rise of the "videogame," as we know it, games have become incredibly lucrative, and that has ushered in a generation of specialist game designers. In the past ten years alone, dozens of schools have started programs explicitly focused on game design. More and more books, talks, and articles are coming out every day that seek to home in on an understanding of the fundamentals of this craft, not to mention serious scientific analysis. In short: it's happening—we're leaving the pre-design era—and that's very exciting.

OBSTACLES

Unfortunately, many of the answers we've arrived at in our pursuit of design principles have been less useful than they could have been due to errors in how we've been asking the question. This should be, of course, an expected part of the growth of any discipline. We branch out in a direction, and it can seem like this direction is working for a long time before we realize some lower-level problems.

A significant source of the problem is that the "founding fathers" of popular modern game design were actually just programmers with cool-sounding ideas. A generation of designers in the 1970s through the 1990s worked really hard to create something special using their ability to program computers to make something that felt like playing *Dungeons & Dragons*, or that looked like watching a movie. And to some extent, they achieved those goals.

By far the largest fundamental issue we've had in terms of advancing our understanding of this craft is our failure to accurately categorize different types of interaction. In short, we've been referring to everything we make—whether it be tabletop RPGs, sandbox simulations, competitive fighting games, or cooperative board games—all as simply "games." With this as our starting point, it can be incredibly difficult to develop some kind of guideline for "good game design." Imagine trying to come up with design guidelines that could be applied to *StarCraft*, *Super Mario Bros.*, *Dungeons & Dragons* and *Dear Esther* all at once, while still having any utility. Doing so is essentially impossible, and this is my explanation for why—with all of the existing books, articles, and even university graduate programs teaching game design—we have very little in the way of game design guidelines that have real utility.

So much of what has been said and written about game design so far is—I'm terribly disappointed to say—useless. There are a lot of "what if" musings, flowery language, and "games in culture" analyses. While these aren't without their use, and we're better off for having them, it's unfortunate that this is all we've got.

If you listen to the modern game design intelligentsia, it would seem as though the problems of actual interactive system design are basically solved: you've got your FPS, your puzzle platformer, your art-installation toy. Now it's just a matter of what kinds of themes we're going to slap on them, or finding new ways to reanalyze the same things again and again.

Most works that come close to being directly useful are extremely low-level analysis that arguably shouldn't even be considered "game design" theory, but perhaps more like psychology or another related discipline. A good example of this is Dan Cook's *Gamasutra* article, "Chemistry of Game Design." In this work, Mr. Cook talks about the basic qualities of *any* interactive system, such as "the feedback loop" and basics about how human beings learn through interaction. He says:

> With the concepts in this essay, you can start integrating this model into your current games and collecting your own data. We've got some immensely bright people in our little market and it is almost certain that they can improve upon this foundational starting point. By sharing what you've learned, we can begin to improve our models of design. What happens if game designers embrace the scientific process and start build a science of game design?

This sort of work is useful in that it allows designers to speak to each other more clearly on some topics, but it cannot be used to help a person design better things. It does not suggest any course of action. Indeed, Mr. Cook is rather open about the fact that his work—like nearly everyone else's in the field—does not provide any answers to people wondering "what should I do?" What he is saying is that this work may be able to serve as a foundation for someone in the future who can hopefully provide readers with something directly useful. But this piece itself, as he says, does not "improve our models of design."

More useful is the work of Chris Crawford, who saw the need to break the great landscape of interactive entertainment into several different categories. His taxonomy goes as follows:

- Within entertainment: "is it interactive?"—if no, it is in the same (unnamed) class as movies, books and films, else it qualifies as a "plaything."
- Within playthings: "is there a defined goal?"—if no, it is a "toy"; if yes, a "challenge."
- Within challenges: "is there an agent to compete against (or the illusion of one)?"—if no, it is a "puzzle"; if yes, a "conflict."
- Within conflicts: "can you impede your opponents?"—if no, it is a "competition"; if yes, a "game."

This is a good first step along the path towards a more useful way to look at design. While it is similar to the taxonomy described in this book, it differs in a few significant ways. To begin with, most of the systems described here—such as "conflicts," "challenges," and "playthings" aren't things that really manifest in the world. How would one go about designing a "conflict," for example? I suppose stealing a co-worker's coffee might be "designing a conflict," but is that really useful to us as interactive system designers?

And that's the problem with today's ideas on design: existing taxonomy is not oriented around understanding the fundamental value and functionality of forms. Instead, what we have are shallow taxonomies created to describe the status quo—only a step or two away from using "genre." The theory and taxonomy in this book, on the other hand, were written to describe the actual interactive forms, at their lowest level. Understanding these is the crucial first step toward building guidelines for better design.

WHAT IS AN INTERACTIVE SYSTEM?

The goal of this book is to improve our models of design, and so, to achieve that, we will be talking only about a specific subset of interactive systems, not all of interactive entertainment (as most current books do).

Interactive systems are systems of rules that humans engage with in order to experience a specific kind of learning. We tend to think of ourselves as engaging with these to have fun, to relax, or even to simply escape. None of those things are wrong, but those are actually less specific and objective than to say that we are doing these things to learn. Even if our intention with a game is to escape, the game works by forcing us to learn.

The word "learn" can also be a bit broad and unclear, so to clarify: with all interactive systems, what we want to do is explore its edges—to understand it. Humans are social creatures that evolved to gain advantages from understanding the world around them better than other creatures do. One useful adaptation towards this end is that learning is thrilling for us. Specifically, when we make a connection about "how something works" that we didn't understand before, we get releases of dopamine that both reinforce the behavior that caused us to learn, but also help us to remember the new information.

So, learning makes us feel good. When a system has something to teach us, and we feel like learning it is within our grasp, we find that exciting or compelling. When it has close to nothing left to teach us (it's been solved), or when the effort required for obtaining what it has left to teach us seems prohibitive, we lose interest—we see that thing as "boring."

Different systems invite different kinds of interaction, and we call these "forms."

COMPONENTS OF AN INTERACTIVE SYSTEM

The smallest unit we work with in interactive systems is the "rule." Rules combine together into clusters that achieve a certain task. These clusters are called "mechanisms," and they are the bits of information in a game that we use to manipulate the game state. Mechanisms may be loosely grouped into "subsystems."

THE FOUR INTERACTIVE FORMS

With this book, my aim is to provide designers with useful, functional guidelines for designing better games. By "games," however, don't think "all kinds of interactive entertainment." Instead, know that it refers to a specific subset of the colloquially defined "games" that, if one were forced to use existing language, might be best described as "strategy games."

In my last book, *Game Design Theory: A New Philosophy for Understanding Games*, I detailed my proposed categories for interactive systems. I've since come to refer to this as "the four interactive forms."

There are four interactive forms that harness the four essential types of play—toys, puzzles, contests, and games. The first thing to note is that these terms are being used with prescriptive definitions; the word "toy" and "game" as they are colloquially known have different definitions than those proposed here.

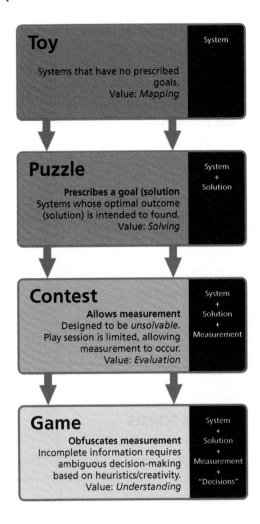

This book is not about these forms in general, it is all about the design process for just one of the forms—the game. With that in mind, it's worthwhile to take a moment to understand the contrast between this form and the other forms.

Toy

The "toy" is simply a bare interactive system. It has rules, including limitations on what the player can and cannot do, as well as objects and variables that can be manipulated by player input. However, it does not have goals, something that is the hallmark of all other types of interactive systems. It is indeed the only form that is goalless.

The toy's primary value could be best referred to as "mapping," or possibly "exploration." Playing with a toy could involve throwing it, bouncing it against a wall, building with it, stretching it, and other exploratory types of acts. When you play with a toy, you are experimenting to find the edges of this object.

A very simple example of a toy is something like a yo-yo. A yo-yo is indeed an interactive system—you can simply bounce it up and down, or you can "sleep" it (cause it to continue spinning at the end of the rope), as well as perform dozens of tricks with it. Finding the various interesting ways that a yo-yo can be "played with" is exactly what toys are about.

A much more complex example of a toy would be the popular PC sandbox *Garry's Mod*. In it, you can create platforms, attach pulleys, weights, rockets, balloons, magnets and other physics objects, not to mention fully poseable character models with physics ragdoll software. You can create crazy situations, from simple stuff like building a tower and knocking it down, to creating a fully functional "Mecha" robot. You can also just pose characters in funny ways and take screenshots.

And doing all this silly stuff with *Garry's Mod* is the point. You can't "win at" *Garry's Mod*, instead you play with it, just like a yo-yo. Theoretically, you can "solve" toys—this would be done by mapping

GARRY'S MOD ISN'T A GAME?

It might be tempting to call something like Garry's Mod *a game, and many people do, and by the colloquial definition they are not wrong. However, it's worth asking whether that's a useful, consistent way to use the word "game" or not. I just demonstrated how* Garry's Mod *has all the properties of a ball or a yo-yo, neither of which would we call a "game." So why is it a game, exactly? Because it runs on a computer? What are the criteria for this other definition?*

every bit of them so that there is nothing left that can be done with it that you haven't done before. In practice, we tend to get bored with toys well before we reach this point, because we can sense that there aren't that many edges left to explore.

Puzzle

One could, of course, prescribe a very specific goal to *Garry's Mod*—even something like "move this platform from here to there." When you prescribe a "binary goal" or "problem" to a toy, you get a puzzle.

A puzzle has a binary success condition, which means that there is a binary measurement happening. Either you solved the problem, or you didn't—zero or one, true or false. No other conditions or state information matter to the puzzle. This is why we refer to this state as "the solution."

As an example, consider the common jigsaw puzzle. Of course, a jigsaw puzzle usually comes in a box, and can contain as many as 1,500 or more small "jigsaw" puzzle pieces, with the implicit (if not explicit) instruction to "create the picture on the front of the box with these pieces." If you have completed the picture, then this puzzle has been solved. There is no other measurement that's happening. It doesn't matter if it took you five minutes or five hours; the objective was simply to achieve the binary success state.

Another more modern example of a puzzle would be a single level of *Portal*. In this system, you usually have to pull levers, hit switches, move crates, and other binary actions that eventually get your avatar to the end of the stage. This "getting to the end of the stage" is the binary goal. If you've done it, there is no other measurement that is relevant;

how long it took you—or even how you did it—isn't important as it isn't even measured by the system.

While all systems that inherit from the puzzle have a solution, only the puzzle is designed to be solved. It's also worth noting that because of this, the puzzle tends to be the most "disposable" of the four systems. After finding the solution to a puzzle—which again, is the goal of interacting with the puzzle—interacting with it ever again (or at least, until you forget the solution) is generally of minimal value.

This will become clearer as we continue through this chapter, but "designed to be solved" is a crucially important concept in understanding not only how different puzzles and games are. A choice a designer makes that may be good for a puzzle is likely to be bad for a game, and vice versa. If a designer is not aware of this concept, he will make worse puzzles and worse games.

Contest

The third form, the contest, is where we actually start to measure things. In the contest, there is some non-binary, meaningful measurement going on.

Good examples of contests would be things like the 100 yard dash, pole vaulting, or arm wrestling—all of which would be physical execution contests, wherein some aspect of physical ability is being measured. Non-physical examples of contests might be something like a "memorization contest" such as the card game Concentration.

Contests can also be single-player, so long as you have something to measure against. The result of a contest—a measurement—can only derive meaning from being compared to something else. Arguably, this is included in the definition—or at least the spirit of the definition—of what "measurement" means. To measure something is to compare it. So for a "single-player" contest, you need some clear, achievable goal. An example could be something like: "can you do 30 pushups in 25 seconds?"

A key point of understanding about good contest design is that they should never be allowed any room for strategy. Those who are serious about contests already understand this. If you are running an arm wrestling tournament, for example, you want to make sure no one is doing something that gives them an advantage over other players, such as choosing to sit in a different pose, or holding the opponent's hand in a new way, or any such thing. In fact, any "decision" you make in a contest would generally be formally recognized as cheating.

Contests, unlike puzzles, should also be designed to resist solution. Puzzles are designed to be solved—so you make the absolutely correct, ideal input, and then move onto a new puzzle. However, contests need to be solution-resistant enough to be able to accurately measure input. For instance, if bowling was played in a set of just one frame instead of ten, you'd have a problem where most high-level players were getting "ties" with the maximum possible score very often. In these cases, the system is not doing a good job of measuring the accuracy of the participants. One player may be significantly more accurate than the others, but the system no longer consistently picks that up. If this were the case, bowling would be a less good—and by good I mean effective at delivering its value—contest.

Game

The fourth and final form is the game, or, if you prefer, "strategy game." Games are contests of decision-making, meaning that what is being measured is your ability to make decisions.

Games are interactive systems (inherited from toys) that contain a goal (inherited from puzzles), and that contain measurement (inherited from contests). In addition to this, they also have some form of obfuscation, usually in the form of incomplete information and/or massive complexity that makes it difficult for humans to identify optimal inputs. This process of identifying more-optimal inputs is what makes games special, whereas other systems such as contests are about executing optimal inputs.

GAME

In this book, we'll be using the word "game" to refer to a very specific kind of system—the "contest of decision-making." Although, in the past 20 years, a common colloquial (at least among those involved in digital interactive entertainment) definition for "game" that includes all interactive entertainment has become the primary usage, this is not the way the word will be used in this book.

The most classic example would be something like chess. Chess is composed of an 8×8 grid board and 32 pieces that have special movement abilities, yet from these simple rules, a giant web of possibility space unfolds that no human can possibly understand the entirety of. Without knowing exactly what they are doing—having incomplete information—players make moves that they think seem rather optimal, although there is always room for debate.

All games are at least theoretically solvable, but as with contests, designers want to make their games as difficult to solve as possible (without causing too many other problems). A game that is easily solved, such as Tic-Tac-Toe, is a bad game. This is distinct from puzzles, which are designed to be solved.

Games and game design are the subjects of this book.

BASE VALUE OF INTERACTIVE SYSTEMS

There is a very important, fundamental atomic property of all interactive systems, which we need a word for. We lack a word for what this thing is in the English language, so we'll have to conscript an existing word for the job. The thing that all interactive systems give you is something we can refer to as "understanding."

The sort of abstract thought that interactive entertainment in general forces people to use has already been heavily studied and is well-understood. Countless papers, articles and books have been written on the subject. One of the most famous is Raph Koster's book, *Theory of Fun for Game Design*.

In this book, Mr. Koster goes through the process of how various interactive systems work. Like most existing texts on game design, Mr. Koster's work does not separate existing works into their forms; instead, he looks at all interactive systems, from pen and paper RPGs, to games like chess, to puzzles like *Solomon's Key*, to interactive fiction, to rhythm games, and everything in-between.

Because of this breadth, it's difficult for the author to provide any insight into how interactive systems really work, let alone prescribe any clear, useful guidelines for designing them. However, he is able to hone in on the one common element in all interactive systems, and that's precisely what his book is about.

What Mr. Koster observed is that all interactive systems are based on learning. When we learn something, when we make a connection we didn't make before, our brains release chemicals that help us to remember this new bit of information, and also make us feel good at the same time. This simple concept—"learning"—is the author's basic explanation for why games are "fun": humans like to learn, and inter-active systems facilitate learning in a safe environment. There are, of course, other elements of games that can be "fun," like artwork, or fantasy simulation, or obtaining status, but the unique kind of learning that games have is their essential property.

The stuff we're learning can be referred to as bits of "under-standing"; we're coming closer and closer to fully understanding this system. Formally, a system that contains no understanding left to gain is considered "solved."

FORMAL BREAKDOWN

In the most technical sense, "solution" is a destroyer of all four forms. Once a system of any kind is solved, it doesn't retain any of its original intended value. For example, completing a level in *Portal* completely destroys the puzzle. It has no puzzle use to that user again, unless that user somehow forgets the solution. This is because it has no more understanding left to provide the user.

Of course, this doesn't mean that the user can't still get some value out of this thing. In the specific case of *Portal*, the user has the ability to create portals that allow the player to do all sorts of crazy, dynamic actions. A great example is placing one portal on the ceiling and one on the floor, and then falling repeatedly between them. Doing this causes the player to build up great speed,

> ## VIDEOGAME
>
> *While the word "game" has a number of different definitions, the word "videogame" really only has one common usage, which means "any digital interactive entertainment software."*
>
> *In this book, we'll generally use the phrase "digital game" to refer to games that operate on computers, and "videogame" to refer to "any digital interactive entertainment software."*

at which point they fire another portal against a wall, which turns their falling portal loop into a player/avatar launcher, and they career across the stage.

Has *Portal* become a toy in this case? It depends on what you mean when you say the word "*Portal*." It's pretty easy to take the components of just about any system and "use it as a toy." You can juggle chess pieces, or you can throw jigsaw puzzle pieces like Frisbees. So certainly *Portal*, the computer application, has indeed become a toy. Or, more specifically, this level in the computer application *Portal* has become a toy.

It might make more sense, however, for us to use the titles of games to refer to a specific ruleset. Each level in *Portal* is its own puzzle; its own self-contained system. So if we get very specific, what we see is that once we solve that puzzle/level, it is effectively dead. Yes, the components can be used for a toy, and it might be a great toy. Further, you can even prescribe new rules that might turn that level into a contest or even a game. None of these points negate the fact that solution has killed the puzzle (level). This can be referred to "breakdown," or simply "solution."

All forms, not just puzzles, are capable of a similar breakdown. A contest has broken down if all contestants are "maxing out" on their measurements. Even a toy can break down—if you've explored everything there is to explore, mapped all of the edges, then there's nothing left to do. Games break down when the decision-tree is solved.

FORMAL BOREDOM

It's worth noting that a system doesn't have to reach a point of total breakdown to have many of the negative effects of breakdown. If a system is close to breaking down—meaning, most of what's there to understand is already understood by the player—that has many of the same practical effects as if the system were totally solved.

Interestingly, there is actually just one reason why people get bored with a system, and here it is: they feel like the remaining understanding is too difficult to access. There are a number of reasons for why a person might feel this way.

- They've actually solved the system, and there literally is no more understanding to be found, no matter how much effort they put in. This would be the case for most adults attempting to play Tic-Tac-Toe. This also is sometimes the case even if the player doesn't know it, as is the case with many highly random games. The player is routinely playing optimally, but the system only gives positive feedback some percentage of the time.
- They haven't quite solved the system, but have explored a significant percentage of its possibility space, and the amount of remaining possibility space doesn't seem worth the trouble.

There are two reasons why it might "not seem worth the trouble." The first one is that there isn't much possibility space left. This is the case almost every time a person stops playing a videogame, most of which have a somewhat low amount of possibility space. Players can detect this, if only subconsciously, and, when they do, they quickly lose interest.

The second reason is when there is technically still a lot of possibility space left, but players would have to do something they perceive as annoying, uninteresting, or overwhelming to obtain understanding of it. For example, many players find it difficult to really dive into the classic, abstract board game Go. This isn't because anyone has come close to solving it—no human has—but rather because the amount of information that players have to learn if they want to seriously understand the game is massive. The sheer huge possibility space of Go can make it feel like anything they could learn would be futile—like trying to empty the ocean with a bucket.

ACCIDENTAL ANTI-FORMS

There are a few kinds of systems that are commonly encountered in both digital and non-digital interactive entertainment that, while technically falling somewhere on the spectrum of the four forms, are not utilizing the structural values of those forms. Instead, they are either exploiting some part of human biology or a spectacle in order to function.

Gambling Machines

The first games that ever became popular, thousands of years ago, were almost all gambling machines. Today, there are the obvious, "admitted" gambling machines, such as roulette or slots, where you are literally asked to gamble money. However, not all gambling machines involve money, and not all gambling machines are pure gambling. Many games that are thought of as somewhat strategic actually have high amounts of luck involved, which ultimately—as we'll explore more later in the book—turns them into gambling machines. For example, there's plenty of strategy to poker, and you don't have to play with real money, but because of the amount of luck involved, most of what's going on is that you're "waiting for a payout." Many "strategy games"—such as the card game Dominion, the board game Risk, or videogames such as *Rogue*—all quickly end up with a situation where players achieve basic competence and then are just waiting for that big payout.

Fantasy Simulators

A fantasy simulator is a system whose true purpose is to simulate some kind of fantasy world. This could be something like a flight simulator, or it could be something like *Dungeons & Dragons*, or a computer RPG. In all cases, the design objective is not necessarily anything related to the actual interactivity itself. Instead, there are other motivations. With videogames, it's often some kind of power fantasy or escapism: you're entering a whole new world, as a brave warrior, or what have you. Some other fantasy simulations are built for educational or functional purposes, such as flight simulators. Either way, in all cases "simulation" applications should be considered tools rather than interactive entertainment, because their value is essentially an extrinsic value, it's not generated by the interaction itself.

Chores/Labor Machines

Often there is some crossover between this and the gambling machine, but the distinction here is that labor machines are machines that you interact with explicitly to achieve an extrinsic goal of some kind. "Grinding" in most RPGs falls into this category, where the player does routine, low-/no-risk tasks repeatedly for a benefit or reward of some kind. In the real world, we often refer to these kinds of things as "chores"—things that you do entirely for an extrinsic purpose and that have no intrinsic value. In the most technical sense, most of these chores are technically puzzles, but they're just very bad puzzles in that they don't deliver the value that we expect a good puzzle to deliver.

Section 2 THE ESSENTIAL VALUE OF GAMES

FINDING VALUE

In order to prescribe any guidelines for how to make good games, we have to first identify what it is that makes a strategy game "good." After all, isn't it ultimately a subjective question? Isn't one man's ideal game totally worthless to another person?

Of course, we can never know what would be ideal for any given individual, in practice. Because that's impossible, let's take that possibility off the table completely. What are we left with? Where, if anywhere, is there room for us to start building a foundation of good game design principles?

While the emotions of a given individual towards a specific game can be incredibly complex and nearly impossible to predict, what we can do is look at the actual functionality of game systems objectively. In this book, it will be demonstrated clearly that a game system actually "works" or "fails to work" in the same way a clock, a bridge, or any other product of engineering does.

To take an extreme example, let's imagine a new rule for chess that replaces the current "checkmate the king" rule:

Capturing any of the opponent's pieces results in a win.

It should be pretty easy for everyone to detect that that's not a good rule. Just about everyone would agree that it's a worse rule, and it could be argued that those who disagree are objectively wrong. Something is objectively worse about this rule. There is, objectively, way less of something with this rule in place, and whatever this is is quite likely also the thing that causes a vast majority of people to react negatively to the rule.

It is not as though "most people just happen to be of the opinion that this is a bad rule." At the time of writing, no poll has been taken to measure this opinion, and yet one could already know with great certainty that almost no one would think it's a good idea. In other words, there is something—some actual, mechanical quality that actually manifests in games—that can be objectively measured. Something consistent in reality is informing our opinions. There is clearly something *objective* about "what makes a good rule."

With my extreme chess example, it's somewhat easy to see, and probably not too contentious. Most people would have the general sense that much has been "taken away" from the game, that the game has become shallow or boring because of this rule. This same objective measurement exists for *any* proposed rule. It's just that it's more difficult to identify and measure in many cases.

Remember that, in a search for objective truth, there is room for individuals to disagree about what the truth is, and this does not negate the fact that there is some "more true" answer that could potentially be found. What might be a little less obvious is exactly why that's not a good rule, and that's where we get into our next section.

DECISION-MAKING

DECISIONS

We need a word that points directly to the kind of decisions that we see in good, unsolved games. For the general concept of a person choosing between several options, let's use the word "choice." For our purposes we'll use "decision" for the ambiguous, heuristic based choice in an unsolved strategy game.

We've already talked a bit about why people like interactive systems—people like learning, and interactive systems facilitate that in a safe, actual-risk-free environment. But why do people like games, specifically?

Of all the interactive forms, games have the highest potential for intellectual value. This is because of the focus in games on decision-making.

Decision-making is an interesting and complicated thing. When is something a decision, and when is it merely an automatic reaction? Sometimes what seems like a decision is actually something that we just knew the answer to and simply entered in the answer. Sometimes, we have no information to go on at all. In other words, not every time we have a choice, do we necessarily have a decision to make.

Decision-making requires that we do not have all of the necessary information needed to make the choice, but that we do have at least some of the necessary information. Having all of the necessary information means that you have solved at least this part of the game. For instance, if you're playing Tic-Tac-Toe as the "O" player, and you see the following scenario on your turn:

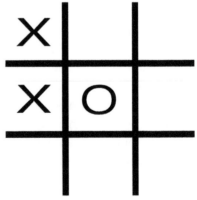

A Tic-Tac-Toe situation

In this situation, it's obvious that you should "choose" the bottom-left hand corner. There is no room for ambiguity or room for debate on this at all; if you don't do this, you'll lose next turn, it's as simple as that. This situation—and actually pretty much all of Tic-Tac-Toe—is solved instantly by most adults who encounter it.

Indeed, it can and should be argued that the "O" player doesn't have a decision to make in this situation. If you know the right answer, then you can't make a decision.

On the other hand, situations wherein a person has no information to go on at all are also not decisions. Take the following illustration, for example. Which door should you choose?

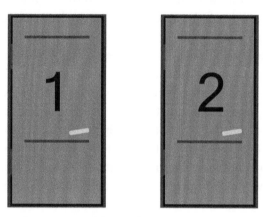

Two identical doors that you must choose between

There's no other contextual information that you can use to give you a hint at which door might be a better option to choose. So, you simply have to guess—make an arbitrary, non-conscious choice. Guesses are not decisions.

Another example of a guess would be if you were asked to "decide" which number will come up when a six-sided die is rolled. Each roll outcome has the same likelihood, so you again must pick arbitrarily.

We can break up the kinds of choices as follows: "solutions" are choices that you have 100% (or close to 100%) of the information you need to make the choice. "Guesses" are choices that you have 0% (or close to 0%) of the information you need to make the choice. And "decisions" are when you have something in-between.

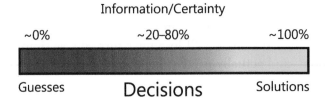

Somewhere between guesses and solutions lie decisions.

Another type of interaction that sometimes gets confused for a decision is actually just a reaction—or perhaps even a "reflex." No one would suggest that when the doctor bops you on the knee, and your leg moves up, that you "made the decision" to move your leg. It just happens.

Similarly, much of the interactions in high-speed real-time games such as *Street Fighter* actually aren't decisions at all, but rather similar muscle-memory reactions. While there is certainly some strategy going on, a lot of it is just measuring how well you trained your hands to do the right thing in all of these different situations. It is worthwhile to delineate between things that are conscious decisions—things we actually intentionally chose and didn't just do automatically—and unconscious decisions, or reactions. The reason is that we have control of, and responsibility for, the things that we consciously choose, whereas things that we do "automatically" or "accidentally" aren't really in our control during a game. The entire premise of there being a difference between contests (pure measurement of a resource) and games (contests of decision-making) is that games contain the possibility for the worse player to win due to his ingenuity or creativity.

WHEN GUESSES BECOME SOLUTIONS

Interestingly, when you are really at zero information (as is the case for choosing between two identical doors or predicting the outcome of a dice-roll), your "guess" is also the solution. If you have no information to go on and must choose between Door #1 and Door #2, the optimal solution—the input that no input could be better than—is to choose arbitrarily. You can do no better (and no worse) than choosing arbitrarily, so choosing arbitrarily is a solution . . . and a guess.

Let's take another scenario. Imagine you're asked to choose a red or blue die to roll. These are special dice that, instead of pips, either have a star or nothing on their faces. The red die has one star, and five blank faces, and the blue die has five stars, and one blank face. The objective of the game is to roll a "star."

In the situation where we had a one in six chance to succeed no matter what we chose, the optimal choice was to choose arbitrarily, and we call that a guess. Now, we have two weighted choices, one where we have a one in six chance and one where we have a five in six chance. How does that change what it is we're looking at?

Well, obviously, a five in six chance is superior, so we're going to choose that—this is a solution. There's no room for debate on the matter. This also extends to other, finer comparisons, such as:

The Queen of Hearts has a 9/52 chance of success.
The Ace of Diamonds has an 8/52 chance of success.

Once you've actually determined the odds of success for two different moves, there is no choice left—it's solved—we should obviously choose the Queen of Hearts. Of course, it's a different story if there are many gameplay factors that make the odds very difficult to calculate.

In fact, you could frame the entire question of "is choice X a decision?" by asking the question "can I accurately calculate the odds of success?" If you can, then it's a solution, and if you can't at all, then it's a guess.

COMPLEXITY

Since humans are so deviously smart, games have to be incredibly complicated in order to avoid being solvable. Broadly speaking, there are two general ways this is accomplished.

Componential Complexity

Componential complexity is usually pretty easy to understand. Basically, componential complexity is complexity placed into the game, manually, by the designer. When the designer adds new rules, abilities, actions, or other components, this increases the componential complexity. Most modern videogames, and even many physical games, have tons and tons of componential complexity.

This kind of complexity is currently so high on a regular basis that it almost goes unnoticed; people are used to it. *StarCraft II*, for example, has roughly 50 unit types among the three races, which already seems like quite a bit, but each of those units has roughly a dozen or more different statistics such as size, shape, armor type, cost, build time, special abilities, energy, health, damage, attack rate, and other unique qualities that define what they are. In other words, each unit contains a lot of componential complexity.

In order to play a game—to form strategies in that game—you must learn all of that game's rules. If you are trying to form a strategy, and there is some rule that you don't know about, then you simply aren't able to form a coherent strategy. So, while all games need to have some componential complexity in order to even exist (rules are componential complexity), each new rule represents a cost to the player. There are other great costs to a system that has too many rules too, which we'll get into in more detail later.

Emergent Complexity

Much has been written on the idea of emergence in interactive systems and, thankfully, it's something we collectively seem to have a pretty good grasp on. The concept itself is simple to understand: put a few components into a system in such a way so that when they're activated, a great number of game-state possibilities emerge.

While everyone agrees that emergent complexity is important, and all games make at least some use of emergent complexity, there are currently too few games with great emergent complexity, which also can be called "elegance." As has been said before, a great game is easy to learn and difficult to master, and that's exactly what elegance describes.

The classic example of emergent complexity is chess. There are just six unit types, on an 8×8 grid of tiles, and yet the game's emergent complexity is enough to keep millions of players interested for hundreds of years.

The quickest way to put it is: when you're designing a game, you want to get the most emergent complexity (unique game-states) you can with the fewest bits of componential complexity (rules). The wider this gap is between the two types of complexity, the more elegant, the more "easy to learn and difficult to master" it becomes.

THE STRATEGY GAME LEARNING LOOP

Let's say you were tasked with the job of having to recreate a perfect replica of your friend's house, exactly as it is right now. How would you go about doing this? Maybe you can go ask at city hall for a floor plan—that would be a great place to start. But that's just the skeleton. We need an exact replica, down to the finest detail—so similar that if your friend woke up there, he'd think he was home.

You'd also need to walk around in his house and start collecting data. What kind of lighting does he have? What kind of furniture? What kinds of rugs does he have, if any? What does he have in the fridge? How does his living room smell? How does his bathroom tile feel on your feet? What sounds can you hear from the garage?

In order to recreate a physical object, like a house, you need to walk around it, touch objects, look at them, smell them, and more. But games are not physical objects. Games are abstract, non-physical structures made entirely out of concepts. Yes, you can touch a chess piece or a PS4 disc, but you cannot actually touch a game itself, for a game is merely a set of rules. For this reason, you cannot touch them, or smell them, or hear them.

The way we touch the edges of a game is by making decisions.

Despite the vast breadth of possibilities in terms of what a game can be, all games follow the same low-level process by which they deliver their value. As was mentioned earlier in this chapter, the basic unit of value in all interactive systems is "understanding," and games are no exception. The difference is in how understanding is delivered.

The basic composition of a strategy game in motion, at its simplest, looks a little bit like this:

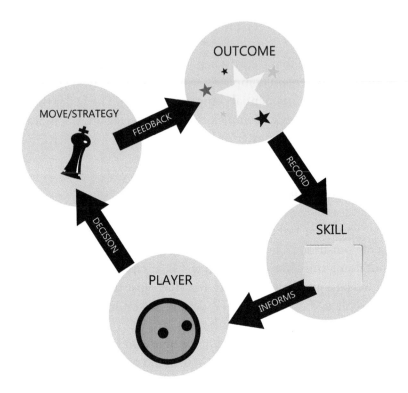

The strategy game learning loop

At the bottom, we have the user. In the game he is confronted with a decision to make. He makes the decision, and enters it into the system using some kind of input method (a button press, a verbal command, a joystick tilt, or sometimes even the lack of one of these things).

The system processes this choice through its ruleset and spits out some result. The result is most frequently a new game-state, but sometimes the result is a win or loss condition. In all cases, the information is eventually informed by the win/loss condition. Either way, the user observes this new game state and compares it with the last state. He also compares it with every other time that he can recall where there was a similar situation and he made a similar input. He mentally files this information away for later use, in a folder titled "understanding for Game X." He'll need it; not only for the next time he plays Game X, but even for the next time he makes a move in this current match.

CREATIVITY

Each piece of that understanding is like a new observation about the house you're trying to replicate. Indeed, the user is building a mental "model" of this ruleset's possibility space. The completeness of this model is a significant part of what makes a person good at a game. A player who has played many games is likely to have a more complete model than a player who has played few. Every time a player must make a choice in a game, they first run it on their little, internal, mental "simulator." In their little model, they attempt that choice, and see how their model responds. Is it a favorable result? Did something happen that they didn't expect when originally making this decision? This is what's going on, over and over again, when a player is sitting and thinking about what to do on his turn in chess. If their model is more complete, they will get more accurate results.

"How complete your model is" is not, however, the only thing that goes into making a decision. There is another aspect to it, which we can perhaps call "creativity"—the ability to consider a wide range of possible answers to a problem. This presents a huge reason why getting good at making decisions is so difficult. We must, of course, build up a large, detailed and accurate model—this basically amounts to memorizing thousands of details about the system and how it works. As this model becomes more and more detailed, necessarily a smaller and smaller range of possible options present themselves to us as potential candidates. As a point of illustration, if a person had a game 100% solved, there would only be one potential candidate that he could consider. High-level chess players know that some openings simply shouldn't even be considered.

Indeed, this quality is the biggest thing that makes one person better than another person. If you have to consider 100 different possibilities for your move, and I, having a better model, already can dismiss 75 of those as not-optimal, then I'm at an advantage. I can spend more time thinking about which of the remaining 25 moves are best, thinking more deeply about each option, whereas your thought must necessarily be more shallow since you are forced to consider so many options.

Sometimes, however, this can be a double-edged sword, especially in very deep games. Although you may be able to write off those 75 moves in most situations, the fact is that right now, on your turn, one of those might actually be the thing you need. It may not be something immediately obvious, either; it may be that 20 turns from now, it will become clearer that you needed it. But, right now, you actually need to temper the messages your model spits out at you.

HEURISTICS

Games that are worth playing are always too complex to build a list of every single possibility for them. Instead, players build a list of heuristics. Heuristics are mental shortcuts, quick and dirty guidelines for play that have been shown to have a generally positive success rate.

What are the criteria, skills, or tools that we use to make a decision that isn't based on our mental model? Sometimes these decisions are referred to as "going with your gut" or "a whim," but those aren't really answers. While we all have a feeling for what creativity is, definitions for the word "creativity" often sound more like a list of synonyms, when what we want is a real explanation of what it is.

Creativity is some other skill, distinct from having a detailed model of a problem. Perhaps one way to look at creativity is the intellectual flexibility—or perhaps humility—to sometimes doubt the validity of your model. The other part of creativity is being able to imagine a new arrangement of the known details into a different model, on the fly. Maybe the walls of the house are made of weak balsa wood, maybe the furniture's all attached to the floor, maybe all those containers in the basement are empty.

Being able to doubt your current model and then to create a new, relatively feasible model on the fly allows a player to make a seemingly strange and unpredictable move. In a multiplayer game, we all know how important that can be. It's possible for a highly creative player to throw off a player with a better model by playing in an unexpected way.

It should be noted that your new model must still be feasible, rational, and use much of the data about the system that you've amassed. The easiest thing in the world to do is to make an irrational or arbitrary move. That's not creativity, that's just chaos. There may be times when creativity can look like chaos, but there are no good players of good games that play chaotically.

FEEDBACK

The second half of the loop could be called "feedback." Feedback is the sum total of new game-state information after having made an input. This is the information that gets stored in our brains that helps us to build our model.

Using the game of chess as our example, we can divide feedback into four "phases."

Instant Feedback

Instant feedback is observed right after making an input, but before anything (such as another player or AI) responds. In a turn-based game like chess, instant feedback gives you no new information. This is because if you move a pawn forward, you now see the state exactly as you had imagined it. Nothing new or unexpected happened; we all have a pretty perfect model of exactly what the instant feedback was going to be, so it yields no information. However, in some kinds of games, particularly real-time games or games with random events, you may be able to observe something meaningful about the game state in this phase.

Response Feedback

This phase occurs just after there is some formal response, either from another player or from the system itself. This is easiest to see in a multiplayer turn-based game, wherein the player would get response feedback when the opponent does their turn following the player's input. So, in chess, I move my pawn up on my turn. Then the opponent moves his bishop to defend. This new game-state allows the player to build a new heuristic—"sometimes, when I advance a pawn here, in a situation like this, my opponent will bring up his bishop."

Players generally are able to build a decent amount of their model out of parts found in the response feedback phase.

Strategic Feedback

We'll talk more about what strategies are later, but for now it suffices to say that a strategy is a series of moves or general "move-types" that attempt to come together to achieve some objective. The strategic feedback phase comes after executing a tactic or strategy. In chess, you might have an opening strategy that involves getting your bishops out and into aggressive positions early in order to limit the opponent's wiggle room and hopefully get him on the defensive early. At some point—perhaps after five or so moves—you'll have executed this strategy. Once that strategy is executed, you can take a look at the board and observe how that strategy ended up working out.

Players build a significant amount of their model out of parts found in the strategic feedback phase.

Final Feedback

Final feedback is observed at the end of the game, when a winner is declared. It is the easiest chunk of feedback to observe, and it is also the most important. Interestingly, final feedback can be very difficult to gain much from without also having experienced the strategic feedback that led up to it. But strategic feedback without final feedback means nothing.

All other feedback ultimately gets its meaning from final feedback—for this reason, we often say that the goal of a game is the anchor point around which the rest of the game revolves.

FUN

All of this technical stuff sounds well and good, but aren't we forgetting about the real reason people play games? The most frequently given reason for playing games is certainly "to have fun."

Well, whether it seems like it or not, what has just been described is how game-fun works. We make choices, we get feedback, we understand better, and this makes us feel good. Exploring the game space, trying things out, being creative—these are all highly enjoyable activities for we humans. For this reason, throughout this book we will use the word "fun" to refer to this experience.

Certainly, there are other things that people like about games. People like the characters, the settings, the graphics, the music, or even some fun flavor text written on the cards. These are all legitimately valuable things that we are not wrong for enjoying.

However, none of those qualities are *essential* to games specifically. You can put characters, settings, graphics, music, and fun flavor text into many other mediums, and they'd have just as much value (or potentially even more sometimes).

As boring as it might sound, the strategy game learning loop is actually the one essential property of games that makes them valuable. Without this, you do not have a strategy game at all. Maybe you need more qualities to make a financially successful game, or a game that your friend Carl will like, or a game that will appeal to Swedes. But if you have a game that has an operational strategy game learning loop, you can know for sure that your game works.

CLOCKWORK GAME DESIGN

This book puts forward a design pattern that will allow the user to create functional game designs that are both deep and elegant. Without the clockwork game design model, designers can spend years playing "whack-a-mole," perpetually fixing one problem and causing three more. This is because of fundamental issues caused by an unfocused and internally conflicted structure, as we'll explore in depth in the next chapter.

CHAPTER 2

ANATOMY

In this chapter, we will explore the parts that make up a contest of decision-making, otherwise called a strategy game. The three primary parts are the core mechanism, the goal, and supporting mechanisms. Some systems strictly conform to this design pattern—in this book, we shall call these systems "clockwork systems." Many systems, including the majority of today's popular digital games, do not conform to this pattern. To refer to those games, we'll use the term "patchwork systems."

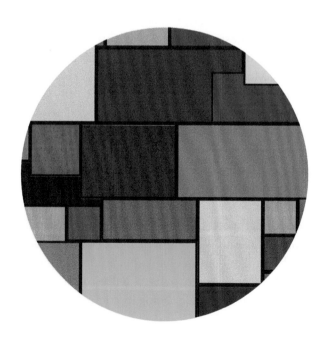

This book advocates for the design of clockwork systems for a number of reasons, all of which will be made clear in this chapter. Primarily, this model is advocated because it gives the designer tools to make more concrete, reasoned judgments about the elements he/she is putting into the game. This design pattern gives a designer the tools with which to pursue elegance. It also automatically avoids a number of large pitfalls in patchwork designs.

Further, a clockwork design is capable of achieving everything that a patchwork design is able to achieve. Because of this, the only reason that one should not follow the clockwork design pattern when designing a strategy game is if they are unaware that the pattern exists. While it could be argued that a patchwork design is "easier" to produce (depending on how much you care about the results), there is no tangible benefit to the final product.

Ultimately, there are no actual advantages that a patchwork design has that a clockwork system cannot achieve. Even the idea that it's easier or takes less time is ultimately not true, assuming your intention is to create something of value. It might seem that it's much easier in a way to "wing it"—to just start "adding stuff" as it seems needed or interesting, it's often *extremely* difficult to design a new gameplay system without using the design pattern I'm advocating (or something similar). Most videogames are designed using a patchwork design pattern, but that works for them only because most videogames don't have original gameplay systems. Most videogames take an established "genre"—which really, is a near-complete gameplay system, ready to go—and then add or remove (but mostly add) elements to that. If all you want to achieve is yet another AAA-style third-person action game, then you can achieve that using a patchwork design pattern. But what you can't do is achieve elegance that way. Elegance can only be achieved by identifying and focusing on the fundamental properties of our medium, and then building around that.

A patchwork design pattern actually isn't a pattern at all—in a way, it's the lack of a pattern. What fills the void where a design pattern should be are things like commercial expectation, a content arms-race, or sheer whim. A strong design pattern is the most significant step a designer can take towards actually being in control of his own project.

Section 1 **PURPOSE**

DESIGN GOAL

When we set out to design something, we have to first start out by laying out exactly what it is we hope to accomplish. Usually, creation comes from some kind of *need* that the author sees that's currently going unfulfilled—"necessity is the mother of invention." While games are not, perhaps, in the same category of "needs" as shelter or drinkable water, "arts and entertainment" in general are something that we value very highly, and rightly so. In this sense, strategy games, the interactive form with the highest potential for intellectual value, have great value to us.

Of course, we already have tons of games. The quantity of games that has been produced in the past five years alone is incredible; we've seen an exponential growth, year after year, in terms of the sheer number of new games being made. But because we're still in the early days of game design, nearly all of our games leave much to be desired.

Our current games take too long to play, often forcing us to play long sessions of games that would likely work best in five-minute sprints. Our current games are too difficult to learn to play, with a dozen or more buttons. Our current games are far too easy to master, with obvious dominant strategies popping up after only hours of play.

Every developer will have his own specific needs that he wants to fill, but we should all be trying to fill the very basic need that's currently not being filled: the need for some truly great games. Games that are no longer (or shorter) than they have to be. Games that are easy to learn, and difficult to master. Games that stand the test of time.

JUMPING IN

Obviously, "I want to make a great game" is not a useful design goal. We need to find a more specific, but still very high-level stated design goal to work towards—something broad, but not so broad as to not be useful.

Perhaps what we want to look for is the kind of decision that we want to make. This can be difficult to conceive, and even more difficult to put into words. Some simple examples would be "I want to choose between tactical moves on a grid" or "I want to choose between two arcs that might intercept a line."

As you can see, there are problems with this approach. First, in order to conceive of such a thing, we already need to have imagined much of our system to begin with. If we have enough data to explain what the choices are and something about the context for those choices, then we've already done something else to get to that point.

The "something else" we did was something I call "jumping in." The beginning of a game design project is, in some ways, the most difficult because it is so abstract and nebulous that it's very difficult to understand and make a map for. For the rest of the design process, I have prescribed clear, useful steps that anyone can use as a lens to help them craft their system. However, the very first steps are necessarily vague. Most times, you simply have to try something to get the process started. For now, it should suffice to say that we need to have some basic "idea" for our game, whether it be a mechanical idea, or an attempt to fill some practical need. We'll get into this more in the next chapter.

THE CLOCKWORK DESIGN PATTERN

Based on the theory established in Chapter 1, this book recommends using a specific design pattern for designing strategy games. Regardless of what kind of strategy game you want to make—a two-player card game, a real-time war game, a fighting game, a team-based first-person shooter, a single-player dungeon-crawler—this design pattern can work for you.

This design pattern is a system of design guidelines, based on a new understanding of the fundamental formal properties of games and other interactive systems. If you use this as a template when designing a new game, you will be working with a game that's easier to design—easier to test, to question, and to quantify. Most game designers already work very hard to make their games great, but this design pattern gives them the tools to work smart—to make sure that their hard work isn't wasted on blind guesswork or trial and error.

CONTENT-BASED SYSTEMS

Often, particularly in videogames but also in certain kinds of physical games, we think of a game as having "content." Characters in an asymmetrical fighting game, levels in a single-player platformer, or cards in a collectible card game. However, this way of thinking about game elements is actively harmful for elegant strategy game design.

The word "content" suggests a couple of things. Firstly, it suggests that the system itself is a "container" for objects—that the system is like a big cardboard box, and inside that cardboard box is the stuff you actually care about: the cards, the characters, the levels, etc. This is indeed how many modern interactive systems are thought about—as mere containers for the content. This approach forces you to maximize content, which means any idea of elegance is out the window. Many content-based systems have massive barriers to entry. Further, it makes the task of balance colossally more difficult than it has to be.

> **STARTING LOOSE**
>
> *While your design phase should end with a strong structure, sometimes it's good at the beginning of the design phase to just try something. Sometimes it's good to throw a bunch of gameplay elements—elements that seem like they might cause something to happen—into a box, and see what happens. When doing this, start with the smallest possible number of elements, and then slowly scale up—not the other way around.*

But beyond that, a content-based system simply has less depth per point of complexity than a clockwork system. The reason for this is that content-based systems depend on inherent complexity almost entirely for their overall complexity. While emergent complexity has the capability of allowing exponential possibility space resulting in potentially billions of billions of game-states, inherent complexity generally has only first-order emergent complexity (if any). The reason for this is that inherent complexity, or content, takes form in a large set of elements who themselves are complex and somewhat detailed. Let's talk about why that is.

Parameters for content in a content-based system have to be at least complicated enough to allow for there to be many such pieces of content. So, you couldn't have "content" really that just had "an integer from one to ten" or "a simple geometric shape" as its parameters, because then you're limited to only having a small handful of such bits of content. Content needs to have several different parameters that can be tweaked to allow for there to be many, many different permutations. Usually, these manifest in "special actions" or "powers" or something similar.

The more complicated a piece of content is, however, the less likely it is that it will be able to be a balanced "cog" in the overall ecosystem. If you have a game wherein cards have eight different numeric stats on their face for different purposes, you might think that this complicated card has a deep web of emergently complex interactions with another card that has eight numeric stats on it, but the truth is that only a small number of those interactions will have any relevance in the game system, relative to the goal. We'll return to this at the end of this chapter.

Section 2 **THE CORE MECHANISM**

THE "THESIS MECHANISM STATEMENT"

A good essay is built off of a clear thesis statement, which serves as its "spine." Every good essay has a clear purpose and meaning, which can be summarized into a thesis statement, so good essay-writers often begin with a thesis statement and build from there. Not only will any university require a clear thesis for all essays, but it's simply common sense: an essay without a thesis is an essay without a point.

In game design, our thesis statement is our "core mechanism"—a central mechanism, action, or dynamic that encapsulates the spirit of what a game is really about at its heart. Often, but not always, the core mechanism is literally the action or type of action that the player uses most frequently in a game.

Since games are inherently abstract, it can sometimes be difficult to verbally explain a core mechanism, but we should take care to delineate between a game that "lacks a core mechanism" and a game whose core mechanism is difficult to describe.

We list a core mechanism in two parts:

- Core action: the thing that you actually do in the system. In *Mario*, it's "jumping." In a shooter, it might be "shooting."
- Core purpose: the reason that you do the core action. Note that the core purpose should not be the same as the goal. Instead, it is a description of what general task your core action accomplishes. In *Mario*, this would be "traversing obstacles."

So while the core action states explicitly what we do, the core purpose states why we do it. The core purpose should ultimately be a description of the basic decision-axis of the game; most decisions should be made with regard to the core purpose.

When we state the core mechanism in full, we combine the two, so the core mechanism of *Super Mario Bros.* would be "jumping to traverse obstacles." Note again that the core mechanism is not "jumping to complete the level." We'll get to goals later and why they are distinct from core mechanisms.

Once we've identified a core mechanism, this gives us a metric by which we can judge the game's other rules. We do this by asking: does this mechanism support the core mechanism, or not? If it does not, then chances are it's something we should consider removing from the game. We'll revisit this in the next chapter in more detail.

Let's take a look at one example for the sake of making this concept clearer: *Super Mario Bros.* While this is almost certainly not a *game* by our definition (most likely an execution puzzle or execution contest, depending on whether you're going for completion or points), it's actually a great illustration of the core mechanism.

CORE MECHANISMS

This is a book about building games, not toys, puzzles, or contests. However, it is certainly the case that all interactive forms, not just games, are at least aided by a core mechanism.

Jumping is the core action in this system. It is used to navigate the terrain—to avoid monsters, to jump over pits, even to reach the level's end flagpole. It is also used to kill monsters, by jumping on their heads. While these seem obvious to us, perhaps less obvious was the designer's choice to allow the player to use the jump to unlock power-ups, by bumping the underside of special power-up blocks that cause them to come out of the top. Even less intuitive is the idea that you can use the jump to smash bricks if you use the Super Mario power-up.

The primary advantage of this design pattern—one action that accomplishes many things— is that it makes the system very easy to learn. Players quickly understand how this jump action itself works, and since most of the actions are derived from this core mechanism, the overall system is easier to learn.

Further, a core mechanism design pattern allows a game system to have a kind of coherence that it otherwise would not be able to achieve. In the same way that an essay built off a thesis statement reads smoothly and clearly, a game system whose rules are built off of a core mechanism has a certain intuitiveness that is not only easy to learn but, in a way, easy to play. There are games that still feel "clunky" to play even long after you've learned the rules. One reason for why this could be is the lack of a clear core mechanism.

A system built using this design pattern has many other benefits, particularly for the design, but we'll get into them more in the next chapter.

ONE-CORE DESIGN

A very common problem, particularly in digital game design, is an unclear core mechanism. Since many designers are not aware of the structural concept or importance of the core mechanism, what often happens is that there are usually several "semi-cores" existing at once, with varying degrees of significance. Perhaps one is the most significant, and therefore somewhat similar to a single core, but there's often enough of a conflict between it and the other cores to cause major problems.

At first thought, it might seem like a multi-cored design might be acceptable, or even desirable. Maybe that makes a game more interesting? We want our decisions to be ambiguous, right? So perhaps having an ambiguous core will help with that?

Unfortunately, that just isn't the way it works. When you have multiple competing cores, balance is impossible. We do, in fact, want player decisions to be ambiguous, but that's a very different from "the meaning of game rules." The meaning of game rules themselves should be anything but ambiguous, yet when a game has two or more cores at once, it's impossible to make game elements support them both. This internal conflict causes a cascading effect of other problems, including making the game dramatically, exponentially more difficult (usually, impossible) to balance. This is especially true if the two "cores" are different enough from each other so as to be distinct.

Further, every game—arguably, every human activity—has just one goal (even if it has other conditionals on that goal). Goals must be, as we'll discuss later, the "ultimate expression" of a core mechanism. It is therefore impossible for there to be two different core mechanisms that both lead to the same goal. We'll get more in-depth on this matter later in this chapter.

WHAT MAKES A GOOD CORE MECHANISM?

There's no easy answer or quick guide to finding a good core mechanism. However, there are some criteria that we can check against:

- A good core mechanism will usually be easy to explain to others. If you have to say "sort of" a lot, or provide a lot of qualifiers, this might be a bad sign.
- A good core mechanism can sound thematic and fun, but still must be rooted in an actual, mechanical action that takes place. So, "stomping on bad guys" could be a core mechanism, but "being a hero" probably isn't, because it's too broad.

- A good core mechanism should describe a single action, not a summary of many actions. So "punching" is OK, but "beating everyone up" is less good.
- A good core mechanism should suggest depth. It should be something that ties to a system in a way that we can imagine could have great emergent complexity.

Examples

Let's take a look at a few examples to help flesh out this concept. Keep in mind: this paradigm is not designed to categorize or judge existing games. It was developed to help us design better games. We're looking at existing games through this lens only for the sake of helping us understand how the lens works.

Here are three systems whose core mechanisms are relatively easy to identify, and more or less exhibit the properties one would expect to see in a clockwork system.

Chess—Core Mechanism: "Positioning to Take Area Control"

In chess, the primary thing—actually the *only* thing—you can do is move units. So it might seem obvious that tactical positioning of units—which are basically objects of area control—is the core mechanism. Everything in the game supports this: the way pawns create these little lattices, the way units have areas that they threaten, and even the goal, which is to tactically position your units in such a way to force the enemy king to have no place left to tactically position himself, supports this core mechanism.

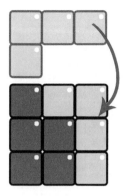

Tetris—*Core Mechanism: "Rotating Pieces to Create Lines"*

Tetris is a simple system—it produces tetrominoes at the top of the well, and they fall.

As they do, you can rotate them, and place them in such a way as to create lines—a solid line of block that fills the well horizontally. When such a line is created, it disappears, and you gain points.

Super Smash Bros.—*Core Mechanism: "Attacking to Knock the Opponent Back"*

If you haven't played the N64 game *Super Smash Bros.* (or any of its sequels, which work similarly), it's a fighting game wherein two to four players are hitting each other and trying to knock each other off the stage—vaguely reminiscent of Sumo wrestling.

For contrast, here are three systems whose core mechanism are much more difficult to identify, and that might be considered patchwork systems.

Civilization

The *Civilization* series is a popular "simulation" strategy game for PC that involves building cities, managing them, moving units around, fighting battles, operating an entire diplomacy system, navigating a technology tree, and several other subsystems (depending on which version of the game we're looking at). The manual says "Build a Civilization to stand the test of time!"—which we might reword as "to survive." But even if we could identify a core mechanism, it is unlikely that any single mechanism really contains "the core action" in such a complex and scattered system.

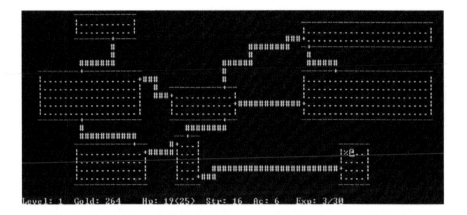

Rogue

Rogue is a top-down, turn-based dungeon-crawling game in which you fight monsters, explore terrain, collect experience points, find treasure, and more. While it's almost certainly the case that fighting monsters is the core action—it is the thing you do most frequently, and doing it is the thing that gives you an advantage in the game—it is not clear if this describes the "decision axis" of the game. Most of the decisions come from choices like, "should I drink this potion now?" or tactical choices like backing up into a hallway to avoid getting flanked. Perhaps the core mechanism is "manage resources to survive"? Or "tactical positioning to win battles"? It's unclear.

StarCraft

StarCraft is one of the most popular digital strategy games ever made. For those who don't know, it involves building buildings, training worker units, getting a resource economy machine going, expanding, building defenses, scouting the enemy, building troops, and sending in troops to fight. Inside a single battle, you can micro-manage units tactically to gain an advantage. Like *Civilization*, there is such a wide array of different actions you can take in this game that it's very difficult to identify any kind of "core." Instead, the unifying element seems to be the "war" theme, rather than anything distinctly mechanical.

Of course, all three of these games are highly beloved strategy games, so it should be clear that a core mechanism is not necessary to create something of great value. However, it should also be noted that all three of these games are quite difficult to learn (not master—simply learning to play at all is hard) and extremely difficult to balance, as they're very content-dependent. The ramifications of this run deep in these systems and incur incredible costs. In the next chapter, we'll talk more about what these costs are.

EXERCISES

1. Write down the name of an activity of any kind. Come up with a verb, based on this activity, which you expect could make a good core mechanism for a potential game. For example, the activity could be "digging a ditch," and the core mechanism could be "moving a shovel to displace dirt."

2. Name an existing game, and try to identify its core mechanism. Explain what it is that makes it the core mechanism of this game. If you can't identify the core mechanism of a game, use it in the next exercise.

3. Name a game for which identifying the core mechanism is difficult or impossible. Propose a clear, new core mechanism for such a game. What other rule changes would you have, or be able to make, with this change?

Section 3 **THE GOAL**

GOALS IN STRATEGY GAMES

We all have an intuitive sense for what a goal is in a game from the perspective of a player, but the goal can be looked at in a rather different way for a designer.

Think of the system as a bunch of parts hovering in space. You have all of your relevant game-state information—a character's health or position, the shape of the level, the time left on the timer, or the direction a projectile is traveling in. All of these bits of information are expressed not through text or computer programming code, but from how those parts are positioned. If one moves up or down, it means it's moving faster or slower. If one moves left or right, it means the player has more or less ammunition.

We can imagine this swirling three-dimensional system of objects moving around as representing an interactive system's game-state in motion. Now imagine another piece that is fixed in space. It does not move at all. In fact, this fixed, unmoving object is the object that allows us to determine the relative position of all the other objects.

This "anchor" on our system is the goal.

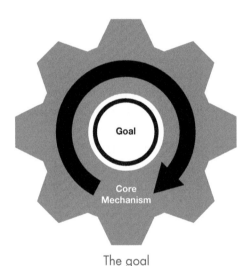

The goal

The goal is the object in our system that gives all other objects their meaning. A rule, a resource, or an action all only mean something in a strategy game with respect to the goal.

Examples

Let's take a look at some examples of goals. For continuity, we'll use some of the same games that we used in the last section, so that it's easy to see how a core mechanism relates to a goal.

Chess—Goal: "Checkmate the King"

The goal of chess is to position your pieces in such a way so that the enemy is both in check (threatened) and has nowhere safe to move to. If you recall, the core mechanism of chess was positioning to take control. Take control to what end? To the end of checkmating the king. A move that gets you closer to checkmating the king (even if indirectly) would be considered a "good move," and one that gets you further from that (often, this means allowing the other player to get closer to checkmating *your* king) would be considered a "bad move."

Tetris—Goal: "Achieving a Target Score"

Most popular versions of *Tetris* do not have a specific score-goal to work towards, but it's implicit in the "high score" model that the player prescribes his or her own score-goal. So if the highest score they got in the past was 110,000, perhaps they'll be shooting for 120,000 this game.

In *Tetris*, we "rotate pieces to create lines," which gets us points. Getting line-combinations in *Tetris* gains us significantly more points, so we want to do this as much as possible. A move that facilitates the gaining of more points, like a neat building of a stack with a single empty hole going down the side, moves us closer to the goal. A move that makes this harder (like getting a single 1×1 hole somewhere in the stack) moves us away from that goal.

In the next chapter, we'll talk more about scoring systems and ways we can improve on the high-score model.

Super Smash Bros.—Goal: "Ring-Out"

The goal of *Super Smash Bros.* is to knock your opponent out of the level. Specifically, there is a bounding box outside the camera's field of view (about 10–20 in-game meters away from the edge of the camera's viewport). If a player travels outside this bounding box, he is eliminated and the other player wins (or scores a "kill"—the game is often played up to a number of these kills).

As we discussed, the core mechanism of *Super Smash Bros.* is "attacking to knock the opponent back." But what exactly does "back" mean? It actually means "towards that hit box," or better yet, "towards the goal."

CLOCKWORK VS. PATCHWORK

In a clockwork system, the relationship between the core mechanism and the goal is patently clear: the core mechanism gets its meaning in the game-state—its "endogenous meaning"—from the goal. As we've done above, you can create a sentence that uses both parts of the core mechanism, plus the goal, to describe a clockwork game almost in its entirety.

In contrast, for patchwork systems, even if you can identify the core mechanism it can be difficult to tie a distinct line between the core mechanism and the goal. This is not so much of a problem in and of itself, but it has many negative ramifications for the player and the designer. If you are following a patchwork design process, it's possible to overlook a total severance of the relationship between your goal and your core mechanism.

Take the PS3 fighting game *PlayStation All Stars Battle Royale*, for example. It's clear that the developers of the game wanted to create a fighting game in the general vein of the popular *Super Smash Bros.*, but with their own Sony-owned characters. So what they did was they copied the entire system of *Super Smash Bros.*—everything from how attacks work, knockback, general stage geometry, down to the smallest detail. As is usually done with such things, they of course replaced the components—the actual characters and moves—and replaced them with their own. That much, the system can handle.

But the developers didn't stop there. Apparently in a well-intentioned attempt to make the game more than just a clone of *Super Smash Bros.*, they decided to actually rip out the goal (ring-out) and replace it with something totally different. Now, instead of trying to knock your opponents out of the level, your attacks give you orbs that fill up a meter. When the meter reaches a certain threshold, you can perform a super-attack that outright kills an opponent—and this is the new objective of the game, kill your opponent. In addition to this change, they also replaced the "damage percentage" mechanism with the super-meter.

So now there is a very strange situation. We still have the same core mechanism—your attacks still deal knockback, and everything you do either moves you or the opponent—yet, actually, movement and knockback now have little to do with the goal. In fact, stages are now enclosed areas with floors and ceilings. This means that when you hit someone, almost none of the information about that interaction matters; or has endogenous value. All that matters was that you connected with your attack, not where you were or where your opponent was. This brings to the game a general feeling of futility.

PlayStation All Stars Battle Royale did not sell well, and it generally was poorly received by critics. Of course, there may be many reasons for why this was, unrelated to this point. Maybe people just weren't excited about the Sony-branded character roster, for example. But it's also hard to deny the fact that most of what you do—the bulk of the information exchanged via the core mechanism—has no impact on the outcome of the game, and this might have had something to do with it.

You do have your patchwork design success stories, such as *StarCraft* or *League of Legends*. Sometimes, even without a strong plan, things happen to fall in place enough so that a game becomes at least playable, especially with constant, frequent patches. The sheer amount of work that went into those games is incredible—these teams had the money to essentially "brute-force" their way to working gameplay. Most of us don't have that luxury—we have a finite amount of man-hours that we can afford to put into our designs before we ask people to start playing them. For this reason, we absolutely need to be working smart, making sure that our efforts aren't wasted. One can only imagine the incredible feats we are capable of when we start putting *League of Legends* kinds of budgets towards developing a tight clockwork system.

QUALITY AND QUANTITY

Qualitatively different goals are easy to observe and understand. Whether it's the goal of basketball to throw a ball into a hoop, to possess the ball for the greatest number of seconds, or to kick the ball into the bleachers are all qualitatively different goals that mean dramatically different things for the system. If the goal of basketball is to possess the ball for the greatest number of seconds, then we might need different supporting mechanisms—players probably shouldn't be able to stand still and hold the ball, for instance. We also might need a totally different kind of playfield and probably some other new supporting mechanisms.

However, there are also quantitatively differing goals. In the case of basketball, the objective is to gain more points than the opponent in an allotted time. For NBA basketball, that allotted time is 48 minutes (four 12-minute quarters), but the international basketball organization, FIBA, uses four ten-minute quarters instead, for a total of 40 minutes. How does this change the game?

The answer has to do with "strategy arcs," which are a series of planned events that result in some larger game-state outcome. An example might be the concept of "getting your rooks out in an aggressive position" in chess. This is a desired game-state that takes some amount of time (turns) to come about.

If a game has any medium- or long-length strategy arcs, cutting down the length of the game might cut into those strategy arcs, potentially reducing the strategic depth of the game. Then again, making the game too long might mean that the game gets repetitive. We'll get into this in much more depth in Chapter 3.

MULTIPLE GOALS

People who are brought up on videogames tend to blend "game end state" and "game loss state"—the classic concept of "game over" suggests that the game is over and therefore you lost. To better understand interactive systems, we should delineate between end-game conditions and goals.

A game may have several end-game conditions that still all point to the same goal. For example, the popular German board game Puerto Rico's goal is "be the player with the most Victory Points at the end of the game." However, a number of events can cause the game to end—running out of worker tokens, running out of available Victory Points, or any player filling up his game board with buildings. Despite having multiple end-game conditions, the goal is still always the same.

What about games that have multiple goals listed? An example is the classic PC game *Civilization*. In this game, you usually have six or seven different victory conditions, most of which are totally unrelated to each other. For this reason, a player really must simply choose one at the beginning, and ignore the rest. Frustratingly, some other player might win because he achieved some goal that you weren't even going for.

NON-INTERACTIVE GOALS

One of the most common forms of goals that we see in all kinds of games, from board games to videogames to sports, is the score. With a scoring system, points are awarded when certain conditions are met. The interesting thing about this is that those points are now no longer accessible by the game. They are essentially external to the game system and cannot (usually) be manipulated in any way. For this reason, scoring systems are an example of a non-interactive goal.

By default, any kind of "race" (which arguably is what a score-based game is, in a way) is inherently non-interactive and more of a "contest" type of mechanism than it is a game type of mechanism, because of how flat it is and how it doesn't reconnect back to the game-state. The common complaint that games with timers—such as most sports—only get tense around the end is because of this fact. The game-state isn't being meaningfully impacted when a player shoots a basket in basketball—all that's happening is that the score is being increased, which doesn't affect anything else.

Health bars are also an example of this. As a counter-example, imagine if, instead of two independent health bars that cannot be manipulated except to permanently subtract from them, what if we just had one shared health bar, with a line in the middle that gets pulled and pushed to and fro. Now this state is one that theoretically could affect the game-state and be a bit of a trade-off point; I'll let the bar come towards me a bit now, and then push it really hard later (an "economy" strategy).

There can be—and in fact are—many great, well-designed strategy games that use scoring systems, racing, or health bars. It's just something to look out for, and an area where we can potentially do much better in the future.

EXERCISES

1. Propose a qualitatively different goal for a popular game: capture the most pieces in chess, deal 200% damage in *Super Smash Bros.*, or fill up the well in *Tetris*, for example. Observe how such a change affects strategy and other in-game elements. Does this change improve or damage the game? What other changes might be needed to support this?

2. Try the same exercise, but with a quantitatively different goal.

3. Prescribe two new goals for chess, without changing any other rules. Play a few games with those prescribed goals. Observe and take note of what tends to happen.

4. Try prescribing a goal to a piece of digital interactive entertainment that currently doesn't have one (toys, sandboxes, etc.). Identify how and why some of these are more receptive to goals than others.

Section 4 **SUPPORTING MECHANISMS**

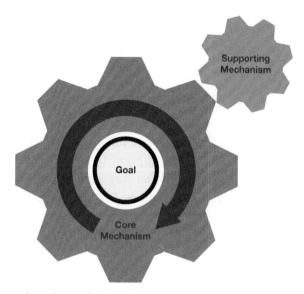

A way to view the relationship between these elements

THE FULL CORE

If the core mechanism is the main action that expresses what the player does in a system, and the goal is the anchor that gives all other parts their meaning, then the supporting mechanisms are, well, everything else. Supporting mechanisms do what you'd expect: they support the core mechanism.

At first, this might sound like a job that is perhaps important, but boring or uninteresting. This is actually really far from being the case. Supporting mechanisms are variables, rules, or other mechanisms that allow a game-state to be nuanced, complex, and difficult to solve. Supporting mechanisms often are the most fun part of game design. In fact, they account for most of the rules that we design.

Once we know our core mechanism and our goal, we can state both of those together as our "full core." So "attacking to knock the opponent back" combines with "ring-out" to form "attacking to knock the opponent back in an attempt to knock him out of the ring."

SECONDARY AND TERTIARY MECHANISMS

There is a hierarchy for supporting mechanisms that should always be followed. Secondary mechanisms are the "first layer" of supporting mechanism. These can be the largest in scope, rules-wise, and must connect directly to the core mechanism. Beyond that, you'll sometimes have tertiary mechanisms that support the core. Tertiary mechanisms should be very lightweight and minor, since they do not connect directly to the core, and some games don't need to have them at all. For the most part, it's safe to say that if you're going even further and creating mechanisms that are even smaller and further from the core than tertiary mechanisms, you might want to rethink adding this rule.

This section will be a bit different than the last two, because once you have a core and a goal, you can start critical thinking about the relevance and importance of various supporting mechanisms. The basic question we should always ask of a supporting mechanism is—and this is probably the single most important tool that this book provides—"does this support the core?" If it does, then it can stay, and possibly be developed more. If it does not, then it should probably be removed.

This connection, however, is not a binary "yes/no" sort of thing all of the time. Sometimes there is a connection, but it's a flat, non-dynamic connection that doesn't provide a lot of emergent complexity in exchange for its cost. Remember—all rules we add to the game incur a cost to your potential elegance! In these situations, you may be losing more by having the rule (due to the inherent complexity cost of having an extra rule or set of rules) than you are gaining in emergent complexity.

GOOD SUPPORTING MECHANISMS

What makes a good supporting mechanism? Of course, the answer is highly sensitive to the context of a given game. However, there are some things that we can say that tend to be good, general qualities for supporting mechanisms to have.

First and foremost, a good supporting mechanism supports the core. Ideally, you'd have just a single supporting mechanism that fully supports the core, and yet delivers a great deal of depth and complexity, because that's the most elegant pattern there is. In practice, this is almost never possible, but as a general rule you want each supporting mechanism to do as many tasks as possible.

In order to do this, a good supporting mechanism is often a "double-edged sword." A good example of this is something like the gem pile height in *Puzzle Fighter*. In this game, as the height of the pile gets higher, you have more firepower to launch at your opponent. However, at the same time, you also are getting closer to losing, as when the well fills all the way up, you're dead (if you've ever played multi-player *Tetris* it's mostly the same mechanism there).

A good "double-edged sword" mechanism will usually have a good (as in, gets the player closer to the goal) and a bad quality for any change to its state. Some very deep mechanisms will have many "edges"—several subtle angles to how they affect the game, some positive, some negative, and some that are difficult to quantify.

So, a good supporting mechanism is like a good anything else: it does the most with the least. It should be simple to learn, yet fold out into great complexity when activated. We'll get into more detail about how this can manifest in the examples, as well as in the next chapter when we actually get into building a game.

Examples

Let's take a look at our reference games and identify some supporting mechanisms, to make the concept a bit clearer.

Chess—Full Core: "Positioning to Take Control in Order to Checkmate the King"

We've already described the full core of chess, but let's imagine that's really all the information we had. We need some kind of game-piece to position on some sort of a space to have positioning, so let's say we're on an endless grid with some generic stones that can be moved one tile in any direction on your turn. Also, the goal requires that one of these stones is the king. This is a bit strange and hypothetical, because there are no existing games that have no supporting mechanisms, as we'll see.

Does this game work? Maybe, but it's probably not going to be nearly as interesting as chess, and it's more likely that it will devolve into degenerate gameplay quickly. What this system needs is some supporting mechanisms.

Chess, despite being a relatively simple game (in terms of its components), has a number of them. One of them is the 8×8 grid board, which limits the distance units can go and allows a player to reduce the territory of an opponent. Another is even the basic, turn-based structure— I move a piece, then you move a piece.

But the most important and interesting supporting mechanisms in chess are the unit types. Each unit type having its own movement and capture capabilities is really what makes chess interesting. So while the basic "engine" framework of chess does indeed rely on the relationship between the core mechanism and the goal, the unit types are really what give chess its identity.

Chess has been through hundreds of years of revisions and changes, so it's quite difficult to find anything in it that doesn't support the core. Although the designers and various custodians of chess throughout the years may not have had a conscious idea of the concepts we're talking about here, polishing a system for long enough will result in a core emerging over time. Weaker rules and mechanisms are eventually removed, even if those in charge don't completely understand why they're removing them.

Tetris—*Full Core: "Rotating Pieces to Create Lines to Attempt to Achieve a Target Score"*

Tetris is a relatively spartan game, so it might be tempting to think that it doesn't have any supporting mechanisms, but if that were true then we'd literally have nothing but rotating pieces to create lines and achieve a target score. That doesn't really make sense.

One supporting mechanism is the random tetromino generation, for instance. While you might at first think that there isn't much significance to this, there actually is. Early versions of the game generated pieces with a very loose random generation scheme—essentially the piece generated just couldn't be one of the last four pieces generated. Later on, the "seven-bag" method of generation was created, where all seven pieces are placed in a bag and then drawn out until all are depleted, creating a very uniform generation scheme.

The uniformity of the generation scheme has massive implications for gameplay. If you've got a *Tetris* (four lines at once) ready to go, sometimes the question comes down to "when will the system give me a line piece?" A version with a less-uniform generator is going to facilitate "high-risk" play, and vice versa.

Another supporting mechanism is the different tetrominoes themselves. We sometimes take for granted the set of seven tetrominoes in *Tetris*, but it didn't have to be that way. There's no reason the pieces necessarily had to have exactly four squares—in fact, other similar games such as *Tetris 2* experimented with different numbers of tetrominoes and even "unhinged" pieces. The inclusion of pieces like this dramatically changes how the game works.

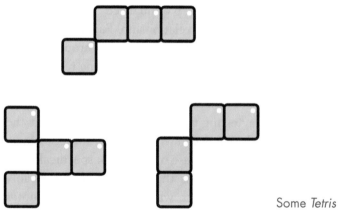

Some *Tetris 2* pieces

Super Smash Bros.—Goal: "Ring-Out," Core Mechanism: "Attacking to Knock the Opponent Back in an Attempt to Knock Him Out of the Stage"

The bulk of supporting mechanisms in *Super Smash Bros.* are the character move-sets. The basic standing attacks, tilt attacks, smash attacks, aerial attacks, and ducking attacks, not to mention the roll and the block, are all there to support the core, to facilitate "attacking to knock the opponent back."

Arguably the deepest and most important one of these is the jump. The jump is an interesting case here, because as you might notice, it does not appear to directly support the core. After all, there is no way that I can jump that will cause my opponent to get knocked back or ring-outed. However, it *does* actually support the core when you realize that it's largely a tool that players use to avoid getting attacked, knocked back, and ring-outed themselves. Further, it is of course used in conjunction with attacks to deliver them, particularly aerial downward attacks when the player is above an opponent who himself is above a pit, spiking him to his doom.

Super Smash Bros. has a lot of moves, however, and it might be possible to question the validity of some of them using this lens. For example, let's analyze the "block" move. This move, when held down, causes a protective force field to surround your avatar, protecting you from (almost) all forms of harm. Does this connect with our full core at all? It certainly does in one way: if you get attacked, you get knocked back, so an ability that cancels out attacks certainly does have some connection to the core in this regard. However, it's not a very deep or nuanced connection—it's merely a binary "allowed/not allowed" relationship. Further, all of the spacial positioning strategy information that's going on throughout the game that informs the full core doesn't really have a strong relationship to "blocking." If you're blocking, you're on the ground, not moving.

So, it's possible that we could at least consider removing the "block" move from the game, and playtesting that for a while to see what the effects are. If it turns out that the game still works well without blocking, then we've improved the game. In the case of the block specifically, it's also quite likely that removing it means that we may (and probably should) remove the "throw" move, which was there largely to counter blocking in the first place. Other than that, throwing is quite similar to normal attacks. Or we could find some other new way to make throws very different from normal attacks.

This is a great example of how the lens provided in this book works—find a mechanism that doesn't necessarily support the core very well, and consider removing it. Doing so might allow you to remove other unnecessary rules as well.

BACK TO CONTENT-BASED SYSTEMS

Now that we've gone over the integral parts of a strategy game, we can discuss why it is exactly that the content-based design pattern is a bad approach. Content, as we stated in Section 1 of this chapter, must be inherently complex. So, while there may be a great deal of complex interactions between two items in an RPG, how many of those interactions have relevance to the goal? Chances are that very few would end up being balanced, and this is also what we observe in every content-based system: only a fraction of the content that's there is viable. Usually it's a fraction between a quarter or an eighth of the total content, and getting it any higher takes millions of dollars and years of man-power. Often, the process of trying to balance such a system, and make more of the interactions relevant, forces the designer to remove what was interesting about the content to begin with. There have been players who complain about games becoming boring from being "too balanced"—this is often what they mean.

If this is true, then how is it that the content-based model has been accepted for so long? The answer is that until recently, we didn't really know that there was an alternative. Sure, people have all played chess and *Tetris*, but games like these often get compartmentalized into a separate "abstract games" folder in our minds. These games aren't the same "kind of thing," the thinking goes, as *StarCraft* or *Street Fighter*. So we don't try to extract lessons from them.

The prevalent design philosophy in videogames still comes from the tabletop role-playing system *Dungeons & Dragons*, in which there is an expression: "min-maxing." Min-maxing is when a player tries to play "optimally"—as in, plays it as though it were a strategy game; and attempts to make the best possible decisions for himself that result in the highest numeric advantages. This isn't how you're supposed to play *Dungeons & Dragons*. You're supposed to play with it, more like a toy, experimenting to find its edges, not necessarily pursuing a goal. Or, you're supposed to "role-play" and do what you think your character would do. Either way, you are not supposed to pursue optimal moves.

This concept carried over into videogames, and it has held us back. We've been affording our game designers a crutch in the form of the knowledge that we will self-regulate. If something is too powerful or boring, then we will self-regulate and just not use it, but that's not really a solution. This creates a kind of "mental dissonance" between what's actually optimal, and what's interesting. It's your job to get rid of any of this kind of dissonance way before the player ever sees your game, so that when he does, he can simply enjoy it. This philosophy of "if players don't like something, they'll just house rule it out" makes it far easier for designers to justify content-based games and other patchwork designs, which seem easier to manage early on, but become impossible to balance later.

Section 5 **THEME**

"Theme" is the word we'll generally use to refer to non-mechanical information that your game uses. Thematic elements are the set of metaphors that we use to explain a ruleset. So, while *Donkey Kong* is actually, mechanically, about "moving through space and manipulating physics to avoid obstacles and reach the goal," the theme would be something like "Mario must save Pauline from Donkey Kong by traversing a tower."

Some games have extremely heavy themes, such as *StarCraft* or *Street Fighter II*. In *Street Fighter II*, for example, the gameplay looks a lot like a "real-life" anime martial arts battle would look. The rules of the game, the abilities, and the restrictions, largely mirror those that one would expect to exist in a "real" battle of this sort—characters can block, they can jump, they can punch and kick, they have health, they can be thrown, they can fall over.

Other games have almost no theme to speak of, like *Tetris* or Go. Sometimes, games with little to no theme are referred to as "abstract games," which, like "abstract art," is abstract in the sense that it does not refer necessarily to any real-world/literal objects. With *Tetris*, there really is no metaphor that you can cleanly attach to it to explain what's going on. It literally is just "arrangements of squares falling into a space that disappear when you form a line." The theme and the mechanics are the same things.

One step beyond that might be something like *Dr. Mario*, which is a similar game in some respects to *Tetris*. In *Dr. Mario*, however, you're dropping "pills" (or rather, Dr. Mario is) into some kind of beaker that's filled with "viruses." Matching pills of the same color with the viruses destroys the viruses. Certainly, *Dr. Mario* is a highly mechanical game, but the theme here does, at least slightly, help to explain how the game works. "Virus + pill = no virus"—most people can get behind that.

THEME AND MECHANICS

With this said, the relationship between theme and mechanics is not always so simple and the line is not always so easy to draw. Theme and mechanics are completely different, yet the relationship is nuanced and important.

To begin, a game is inherently mechanical. There are debates about whether theme or mechanics are more important, but for games— for contests of decision-making—the matter is completely settled. Mechanics—rules—are what makes a game a game. They are its essential properties. As we discussed with games like *Tetris*, Go, backgammon, or checkers, there are plenty of games that have no theme at all. However, there are no games with no mechanics. A game without any interactions is not a game—in fact, it is not even an interactive system. So there should be no debate here, especially given the prescriptive definition for "game" given in this book.

The ultimate purpose of a theme is to explain your mechanisms. Themes are like packets of free information that you can slide into your game that will almost magically have your players understanding what things do. For example, take a card game where each card can be "played" and does a certain action.

If you call that card the "Hammer," that comes with a bunch of expectations. We expect the Hammer to do something like:

The Hammer card

- ■ flatten
- ■ crush
- ■ attack

We do not expect the Hammer to do other things, such as:

- ■ heal
- ■ dig
- ■ diplomacy

For "heal," we might use something like a medical "+" shape or a Band-Aid. For dig, a shovel, and for diplomacy—well, that's an example of where it gets a bit more complicated, but we'll get back to that.

For the most part, you want to choose a theme that expresses the meaning of your mechanics. If this is the case, and you hand someone a Hammer card, they already have some expectations for what that thing is going to do, and those expectations are indeed correct.

So, a good use of theme is crucially important. Remember, the old mantra is "easy to learn, difficult to master"; well, a good, clear and fitting theme is a significant part of how easy your game is to learn.

UNNECESSARY THEME

As an aside: not all themes have a gameplay mechanism that they express perfectly, and not all gameplay mechanisms have themes that express them perfectly. That's OK! Don't feel the need to jam a theme into your game just for its own sake. There are some gameplay mechanisms that are incredibly hard to add a theme to—the classic board game Go is an example of this. How do you express that theme? What exactly is happening? Perhaps an example could be that they are soldiers fighting in a war, but . . . that really doesn't help you at all. If this were the case, our theme is actually suggesting all kinds of things that the game mechanics don't do.

> I have a soldier? OK, I expect he's going to shoot. He doesn't shoot? Oh, OK. Well does he move around? He just stands there, oh, OK—I'll

try to remember that, that's sort of strange. Well, at least I do expect that I'll be destroying the enemy army throughout the game, right? No—in fact, the enemy's ranks will mostly only increase in size as the battle goes on? OK . . .

This is the kind of mental gymnastics that a person has to endure when playing a game with an unnecessary, tacked-on theme. Having no theme is far better than having a bad theme.

WHAT MAKES A GOOD THEME?

As you might expect, there aren't any hard rules about what makes a good theme overall—only what makes a good theme for a given title.

While games are primarily and essentially contests of decision-making, games are also pieces of culture. The theme you choose will not only influence how people play your game, but it will also change who plays your game. This aspect of theme-design is somewhat outside of the scope of this book, but it should be noted that a theme's most superficial qualities may have massive impacts on the success of your game. While a strong clockwork system determines whether your game works or not, oftentimes whether your game actually reaches anyone may be determined by things such as:

- Is the in-game artwork created using pixel art, or 3D models?
- Is the setting a modern warfare setting, or in a suburban backyard?
- Are the characters cutesy, chibi anime characters, or dirty, depressed killers?
- Is the music 8-bit chiptunes, or licensed pop songs of the 1970s?

This book can't tell you what sort of theme, in this regard, will best get your mechanical message across, and neither could any other book. So I recommend letting the mechanics guide you.

There's a lot of motivators out there pulling designers towards making all kinds of themes. Some themes sell better, some themes are romantic for the designer, and some themes are culturally problematic. First, identify what your mechanics' optimal thematic setting would be, and then decide—consciously—what concessions you must make to satisfy other personal/business goals. The purpose of this book is, again, not to instruct you on the best thing to do for your business/personal artistic identity, but rather to make sure you are aware of any costs you're paying for meeting those goals.

Section 6 **DOCUMENTATION**

If you've made the greatest game of all time, but no one knows how to play it, then it may as well not exist. It'd be nice if we, the designers, could be there to teach people how to play our games in person, but since that's not possible, how can we do it? Every game needs to have some kind of documentation that facilitates players learning about how your game is to be played.

Many of us raised in the 1980s to the 2000s are quite likely to underestimate the importance of such documentation. Many applications created during this time were only subtly different from others we had played before, and so forced tutorials started to get very negative reactions out of people who felt—often rightly—that they could figure it out if they were allowed to just play. Similarly, manuals have become almost passé—things of the past that aren't needed anymore. Modern games either don't have a manual at all (for instance, if they're a digital-download-only game) or, if they do, it contains mere technical information (like a legalese protection clause about the app potentially causing seizures) and perhaps a light introduction.

This is only the case because game designers have been failing to do their job. If designers were designing new systems all of the time, it would go without saying that manuals and/or tutorials would be absolutely necessary. A clear, existing example of this is the world of designer boardgames, where everyone accepts that, in order to play, you have to first read through the manual. Designer boardgames often have thoroughly original rulesets, so there's no way players are going to be able to figure out how to play them without going through the (sometimes rather arduous) task of reading the manual.

MANUALS

Game manuals are often very difficult to read. This is because of the fact that manuals use language, which is linear, to describe a non-linear machine. As a point of contrast, let's look at the form of a story. A story is comprised of a linear set of events over time. It's rather easy to place story events in sequential order in sentences and paragraphs and have your story be clear and understandable for a person to read.

Games, on the other hand, are a complex and non-linear web of information: a goal tied to a core mechanism tied to dozens of supporting mechanisms that may have complex relationships. This means that, especially near the beginning of the manual, it's almost impossible to describe what any one element means or how it works—it's all contingent upon other understandings about the system. So in a way, the only person who can really read and understand a manual is someone who already knows how to play!

In practice, trying to learn a game from a manual is hard. You often have to read the manual once through, after which you come away with a "half-understanding" of sorts. Then you might try to play a learning game, where you attempt to go through the motions of activating the rules, frequently bouncing back and forth between the manual and the game. Eventually, it clicks, and then you only ever need the manual again for perhaps some specific, hard to remember number (a common one is, "wait, how many cards do you start with?").

Overall, a manual is perhaps not the most advanced method of teaching your game, but on the plus side, they are very good for reference. Recently, digital manuals are becoming more common, with online wikis being a popular choice. A great quality about wikis is that not only are they nicely indexed and easier to find things in than it would be in a paper manual, but also they're editable. This means that you can edit the wiki when you make post-release changes to your game, and it means that the community can edit the wiki to add to a section such as a "strategy guide" or a "walkthrough."

TUTORIALS

As it was stated in the last section, tutorials get a little bit of a bad rap, largely because of the fact that for many modern videogames, they simply aren't needed for many players and, worse, they're often forced in those very same games (meaning, they can't be skipped; you have to complete them to gain access to the actual game). However, a smart tutorial is still one of the better ways to teach people your game. Of course, this section generally only applies to digital games.

A tutorial is a section of the game with extremely limited functional capacity. Often, you can only do the one thing that the system wants you to do. For instance, the game might be teaching you about your basic attack. "Press A to use your basic attack," the game says, and it won't respond to any other inputs you might make. You can't run off and do something else, or hurt yourself. You're on rails, and you just have to press A to continue. Usually it will continue in this pattern until a good chunk of the game's mechanisms have been introduced.

There is a lot of debate about how to implement tutorials in games. One generally accepted bit of wisdom is to, wherever possible, opt for a "silent tutorial." A silent tutorial doesn't rely on boxes of text or voiceovers to explain rules; instead, it simply sets things up in such a way so that the thing you're supposed to do is implicit.

One of the best examples of a silent tutorial is the first level of *Super Mario Bros*. It starts off with Mario on the far left of a path, already suggesting to the player "you move to the right in this game." Then there is a monster (a Goomba) that comes onto the screen, suggesting that you should perhaps jump to avoid him. Doing so is very likely to cause you to bump the "?" block, thereby demonstrating to yourself that bumping these blocks yields power-ups. Even tiny graphical elements help paint the picture for the player. The shape of the Goomba is bulbous, as though it's something that could be flattened. This suggests that perhaps you can jump on Goombas to flatten them.

Often, you can transition from a non-silent tutorial to a silent tutorial, which transitions to gameplay. For example, you might have the first couple of "levels" in your game be a forced non-silent tutorial, which gives players the very basics of interaction. Then, you have what looks like the real game happening, but it's still limited in such a way that it will facilitate

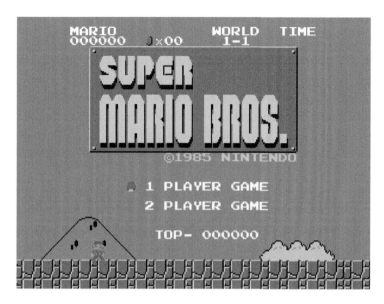

Super Mario Bros.

putting things together. This is actually very common in modern video-games, where sometimes arguably half or more of the game could be called "tutorial"—simply learning what stuff does, rather than necessarily becoming good at using the stuff.

Doing a silent tutorial like that often won't be possible for games with more complex rules, however. If you need to do a "non-silent" tutorial, there are still huge questions as to how to do it. One big question is—should you force players to do the tutorial, or should it be optional? People may be accustomed to being able to figure games out, so if your game is highly original, it might be a good idea to force the tutorial. It's easy to imagine players quickly getting frustrated with such a situation, especially if we're talking about something like a mobile game where patience tends to be on the low side. Games that are bigger commitments, like big-scope, expensive PC or console games might allow an optional tutorial, since players have already largely committed themselves to playing the game just by owning it.

VIDEOS

One of the more innovative, and probably more effective ways of teaching your game, might be with a video. Film yourself, or a more charismatic friend, playing the game and explaining what you're doing as you're doing it. This is an easy way for viewers to pick up on some basics about the rules to your game, but it's also a great way to show players an example of advanced play. Sometimes the best way to use a gameplay video like this is to have one of your best players create a video that's designed to be viewed after players have already learned the rules. So first they learn the rules, and now they can see someone really doing great. This allows them to see the potential for depth in your game's play. It's not quite as good as actually being there to teach a person, but it's probably the second best method overall for introducing people to a game.

EXERCISES

1. In what ways other than those listed in this book could you conceivably teach a person how to play a game?
2. Practice teaching games by finding some more complex European designer board games and teaching them to friends (Puerto Rico or Bohnanza might be good examples to start). What seems to work best for you?
3. If you haven't done so before, find some free wiki software on the web and build a wiki for a game you're designing. Try to organize the information for your game in a way that's easy for a reader to follow.

CONCLUSION

One nice thing about the entire process of trying to teach someone your game is that it's yet another way that you yourself have to look critically at your own work. It's often when you're sitting down watching someone try to play something that you realize which of your rules are strange or difficult to understand. Sometimes, a session of teaching a player how to play your game can inspire a dramatic change in the game, and usually it's for the better. Again, you can make the deepest game in the world, but if no one can figure out how to play it, all that depth is wasted.

In conclusion, there's always the question of "how are you going to teach people your game?", and, ultimately, the right answer is often "all of the above." Create a tutorial, and likely make it forced if it's a mobile or web game. Create a physical manual if there's a physical version of your game, perhaps labeled clearly with a date and a version of the game, since your rules will be changing over time. Make a public wiki available to people. Create a video (or series of videos) of yourself playing your game to show people what the strategy of your game looks like.

CHAPTER 3

CONSTRUCTION

For creators, there's a simple value to creating something. The feeling of having made your mark on the world is very compelling, and it draws many to the act of creation. In a way, creation is a method for achieving "eternal life"—to leave behind some part of us that will exist long after we're gone.

These reasons for engaging in creation are legitimate. In fact, there are many different motivations for creation. Perhaps you want to improve in your craft. Maybe you need to get something off your chest or use the act of creation as an emotional release. Maybe you simply want to document something about your life through your creation. Perhaps you want to obtain a certain social status, and creation is the way to achieve that. Maybe it's just something to do with your free time, to keep your mind limber, or to keep you out of trouble.

All of these reasons for engaging in creation are totally legitimate. Creation is often a great way to achieve these goals. However, everything changes the moment that you ask even a single person to take time out of their day to consume/experience your work.

Once you've asked a person to check out your creation, and they accept, you are now in debt to them. They have now given you a bit of the most precious and irreplaceable resource human beings have— time. In addition to this, they are also devoting energy to the cause of processing your creation. For most creations, there is a gap between the time that a person agrees to consume your work and the moment that they begin to get anything back for it (this is particularly true for games, which need their rules to be explained and understood before they can be experienced).

So what do they get back for it? How can you pay back their debt to them? In a word, by delivering "value." For games, this value can be called "understanding," as we discussed in Chapter 1. A good game provides a huge mountain of understanding for the user to climb, each step along the way an enriching and interesting journey through a rich and complex world.

It is an act of arrogance and disrespect to create something purely for your own purposes, and then ask others to take time out of their day to look at it. If you have created something just to hone your craft, and not necessarily to deliver values to others, that's great—just keep it to yourself (of course, showing someone who has asked to see your work for academic/curiosity purposes is fine—they're aware of the transaction they'll be making).

Because of the debt that we, the creators, are immediately in the moment that we ask someone to observe our work, it's important that we ask for the smallest amount of time that we possibly can.

This is why we pursue elegance. When we give a person an elegant thing, the cost to them is relatively small and the benefit is relatively large, meaning that this interaction has been beneficial to them overall. In this situation, we have done a great thing for another person—we have enriched their lives. A great game designer who frequently makes elegant things provides a great service to humanity, making the lives of millions of people better. Hopefully, the reasoning for why this is preferable to being a person who imposes on others is self-explanatory.

Section 1 **THE APPROACH**

FILLING A NEED

To provide value for people, it's not sufficient to simply be elegant. Elegance is a description of the vehicle that delivers the value, it is not the value itself. In order for your game to have value, it has to fill a need.

For instance, let's say someone designed a board game with the following qualities: it has an 8×8 board, and two armies, each controlled by one player. The armies are the same armies that are in the game of chess, but each player has one extra pawn that goes in in front of their king's pawn. Let's call it "Chess X."

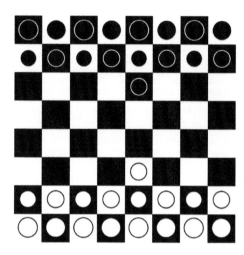

Chess X

This is a game that might be every bit as easy to learn as chess, and quite difficult to master, but, at the end of the day, the world doesn't really need this game. Regardless of the fact that it's probably a lot worse of a game—even if we accepted that it's as good—it's too similar to the existing game of chess, which everyone already knows and can play.

Even if we were to add a bunch of features, instead of remove them, that might not be enough. For instance, maybe we could give the different pieces special powers. White knights get to move a single tile after making a capture. Black bishops can only move two tiles at a time, but can only be captured diagonally, etc. Those examples are probably horribly imbalanced, but let's imagine for a moment that they aren't, and call that game "Chess Y."

Theoretically, both Chess X and Chess Y have the potential to add something to chess, but both games are ultimately a lot like chess, and have a lot of the same kind of gameplay value. They both have the same core mechanism, similar supporting mechanisms, the same goal, and the experience of playing them is quite similar.

So if everyone already has the original chess, and you introduce them to Chess X or Y, it's fair for that person to take the value your game officially provides, but then remove all value that was in the original chess, because the player already has that value.

As an illustration, we can see that to a lesser extent this is true with the games *StarCraft* and *Warcraft III*. The popular real-time strategy

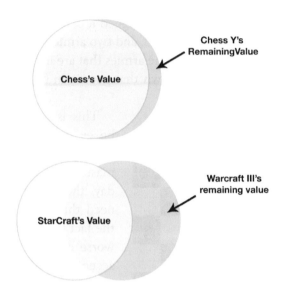

Chess Y's
RemainingValue

Chess's Value

Warcraft III's
remaining value

StarCraft's Value

Chess's value removed from Chess Y's value

game *StarCraft* cuts into its successor, *Warcraft III*, which has much in common with *StarCraft*. Then again, *Warcraft III* introduced many new gameplay elements, such as heroes and AI-controlled monster camps. As *Warcraft III* brings a good bit to the table of its own, so its "remaining value" is somewhat high.

In other words, if your game is very similar to another game that's already existing, it is literally losing giant swaths of its value, since people already have access to most of what you're offering.

To be clear, there are examples where a person takes an existing known system, makes a few changes, and these changes happen to throw the system into a new state of balance that multiplies the depth of the game exponentially. In these situations, even though the rulesets might look somewhat similar on paper, when activated the experience will be dramatically different. So it is possible to "change a few things about an existing system" and still provide significant value, if your changes have massive ramifications.

To give an example of that, imagine that the very first version of *Tetris* showed the player the next ten pieces that would be produced. A year later, a person came along and created *Tetris X*, which limited the piece-preview count to just one. Since in the original version, there was never any potential for "risk-taking play," *Tetris* X might have tremendous value, despite being nominally similar to the original *Tetris*. The original value is "overwritten" and the new value is added.

With this in mind, innovation is not necessary for its own sake. Being original or innovative is not just something you do for "bonus points." Creating an original thing fills a totally unfilled hole, thereby accomplishing the most. Being innovative actually makes your job—filling a need—way easier!

Of course, this point is directed only at a person intending to start a new design project. If you have already finished a game, then it is often highly effective to continue to improve on your existing work. In addition to this, you, as the creator, owe it to the people who have already spent time and money on your work to make sure that it is the best it can possibly be. But if you're starting something new, you don't have this restriction, and you can gain more by doing something that fills an unfilled need.

RULE EVOLUTION

Throughout the entire development process, things will likely be "in flux." At first, you might have some basic idea of what the game should be like, but then upon testing with a rough prototype, you realize that that doesn't quite work the way you had hoped, or maybe you stumble onto something that's even better than what you initially had in mind. This is all a normal part of the process.

Remember that what you're trying to do is a pretty amazing task: you're trying to create a machine that sits on the fine line between "something that's easy for people to solve" and "something that's easy enough for people to learn, but practically impossible to solve." Finding that balance is incredibly hard, and it can take years.

Depending on your particular arrangement, you may or may not have the flexibility to actually follow a game where it needs to go. Whether you're a struggling indie with a band-sized team or a massive AAA studio, there are always real-life limitations.

So, what you should do is take the fluidity of game design for granted from the start. Consider that halfway through, or even 90% of the way through, you might have to make a major shift. You might have to throw out expensive artwork. You might have to remove some feature you spent months balancing already. While the clockwork design pattern will dramatically minimize these kinds of delays and restructurings, you should still factor these kinds of things into your scheduling to begin with.

If that sounds kind of crazy, it's only partially so. In a way, no one really has the capability to see a game through. It takes years. But there are two things to consider that make the prospect more realistic.

The first thing is that you should plan for repeated failures. Whatever the budget is for your game (whether in time or in dollars), allocate between 70% and 90% of that time for "failing"—for following a dead-end path. Remember: each dead-end path is actually one more pillar of strength holding your final ruleset in place. It's much like "rule-evolution"—a rule in a very strong ruleset contains within it the shadow of 1,000 dead ancestors from which it evolved. Players will see your rule, and wonder "hmm—maybe it should have been a different way? Instead of X, perhaps it should have been Y." After some deeper thinking, they might realize that actually, there is a reason it's not Y. And indeed, Y was already tried, and it didn't work.

The other thing to remember is that you don't have to be "finished" completely by the time you release. Even if a game takes ten years to really finish fine-tuning, it's likely good enough to release to the public after just one or two years. And nothing is better for finding flaws than exposing your game to millions of players who are trying to break it.

FINISHED

When is a game really "finished"? Arguably, a game is never actually completely done. Even once it seems done, you could always continue to make little adjustments, add more polish or feedback, or other refinements. Even once the game has been released to the public, you're going to want to release patches and possibly even new features as needed.

It's better, probably, to not use the word finished at all. Instead, think of the game as reaching certain milestones. One milestone is "good enough to be released to the public." It's up to you to decide when that is, but in many ways, this milestone is only the beginning.

ELEVATOR PITCH

A great way to start a project is with an "elevator pitch"—something that's short enough to tell someone about in the time it takes to ride in an elevator with them. Usually, this is anywhere from two to four sentences that describes your game idea in a nutshell. Note that this is not the same thing as a "core mechanism," although your core mechanism may be included in the elevator pitch. Here are a few examples:

Foggy Cavern Deluxe is a game where you're exploring a foggy, dark cave. There is lag between the time that you make inputs and when your avatar responds, so you have to use various cues to know when to turn so that you don't fall into the water or impale yourself on a stalagmite.

Elevator Urchin Dive is a game wherein players race down an elevator shaft trying to catch sea urchins, while also trying to ram each other into the walls. If you touch a wall, you drop a sea urchin. When both players hit the bottom of the shaft and die, the player with the most sea urchins is the winner.

Fancy Portrait Trader is a card game where three to five players play portrait cards to the table and can trade them with each other for money. Players can bluff about how much money they paid for a portrait, causing other players to either have to continue the lie, or call it out at great potential cost.

These pitches are similar to a "statement of purpose." They give you an initial guiding concept to work towards throughout development. On a practical level, they can also be used to help get teammates, fans, or investors interested in your project.

It's almost always the case that if your elevator pitch has to be more than two or three sentences long, your design itself is likely fundamentally too convoluted. Whereas, if you are able to express it in just one, and it still sounds interesting, this might be a great sign.

Here are some examples of bad elevator pitches:

"It's like *Angry Birds*, but the birds are otters instead!"—this is a bad elevator pitch because it doesn't tell us anything about how the game is mechanically different from *Angry Birds*.

"I want to make a game about Az'dael, the half-elf witch huntress who needs to find her pet otter, who has been kidnapped by the Skull King Gul'Thalas, and who . . ."—and so on. These kinds of story/theme/setting/character-based descriptions really tell us nothing about the actual game itself.

FINDING YOUR CORE

It's likely that you will go through many core mechanisms before finding one that ultimately works, and because the core is so inherently tied to everything else in the game, making changes to the core later in development is prohibitively costly. For this reason, you must be as certain as possible of your core as soon as possible. Indeed, finding the right core is likely the most difficult aspect of game design, and it's one of the main reasons why most games aren't very good. At almost every stage of game development it can be difficult to know if your core mechanism is working or not. Sometimes, it seems like it is working for months before you realize the fundamental flaw and end up having to throw out all of that work. Often, even if you have a core mechanism that will work, it can seem like it won't until all the supporting elements are just so.

For this reason, game design really requires the ability to envision how something is supposed to work, and the confidence to pursue it. On top of that, it also requires a great flexibility to be able to throw out months or possibly years of work when you find out that the current direction isn't working.

Now that you're sufficiently scared, it's time to take your elevator pitch, designed to be heard by humans and therefore written in English, into the language of interactive systems. Let's look at the examples from the last section and see if we can come up with some possible cores.

Foggy Cavern Deluxe—perhaps if this game is about using cues to know when to turn, maybe it's a process of deduction? Deduction, however, tends to not facilitate that much decision-making, since it's really just a matter of removing some options and then guessing between the remainders (unless there is only one remainder, in which again, no "deciding" will take place). Perhaps, instead of deduction, you get better at recognizing the "meaning" of certain shapes, in an emergent, non-memorizable sort of way (similar to how shapes have meaning in Go). So in that case, at each turn, you'd see some configuration of rocks, and have maybe ten seconds to analyze it and make a decision. So our core mechanism could be "choosing between patterns in order to traverse a certain amount of distance."

Elevator Urchin Dive—this game has obvious parallels to fighting games. Perhaps we can take some of the "positioning" elements from games like *Super Smash Bros.* as part of our core. It seems that there are multiple motivating elements enticing the players to be in different places at different times, and perhaps the player who is better at evaluating the strength of various potential positions will have an advantage. Our core, then, could be "changing positions to obtain the most sea urchins."

Fancy Portrait Trader—it seems that this is a good example of a game whose core mechanism might be difficult to identify. Is the core mechanism "bluffing?" Bluffing seems like something that happens outside the actual game rules, and anyway still seems reliant on valuation as the actual mechanical skill. Is there an element of memorization? Possibly, but memorization isn't our friend when it comes to creating an atmosphere conducive to decision-making. If players are able to just memorize an answer that works, then no decision needs to get made. Perhaps the core mechanism is simply valuation again—being able to understand the value of certain cards at certain points in the game. A high-value money card might have more value early in the game, and high-value paintings might be worth more later in the game, but in between it gets difficult to know. So, we could try something like "evaluating and trading money and paintings to obtain the most wealth."

"EVALUATION" VS "VALUATION"

The word "valuation" comes up a lot in the world of game design, which can be confused with the common word "evaluation." Evaluation is a general, broad assessment of the overall quality of a thing, whereas valuation tends to be describing a more solid, quantifiable value. So, the result of an evaluation might be something sounding like "it's excellent overall, very few flaws," whereas the result of a valuation might be something like "it has a monetary value of $33."

Obviously, in all of these cases, we don't have anything like a complete game. There are supporting mechanisms, and more specific goals that need to be developed in order to have a complete game design idea. Most likely, none of these ideas would work when actually applied; they are just off-the-cuff examples designed to highlight the process rather than actually be useful ideas.

The common element here is that we're staying abstract. We're not thinking thematically. For example, for *Elevator Urchin Dive* a more literal interpretation of that concept would be that you actually drop cards on the table from a distance, or that you bop little urchin toys around. There may be something to these, but you're far more likely to find something useful when you think mechanically, because you're thinking along the lines of what the system needs, rather than along the lines of what supports the metaphor. Remember that the theme is only there to communicate the system to the player; it is not the system itself. So, finding elements that match the theme and not the mechanisms they represent is like trying to match two jigsaw puzzle pieces together that don't fit.

FINDING SUPPORTING MECHANISMS

Once you have a core mechanism that doesn't seem immediately terrible or obviously flawed, you can move onto the next phase of design, which is to come up with the necessary supporting mechanisms.

As we discussed in the last chapter, supporting mechanisms are there to provide context and add the necessary depth to the core mechanism. For this reason, they each individually should generally be lighter in complexity than the core mechanism. They should provide the backdrop that guides play in the ways you want it to happen.

To illustrate, let's take our example games and run through a potential process for figuring out some supporting mechanisms. Keep in mind that these are all untested, first-draft brainstormed ideas that would almost certainly not work as stated!

Foggy Cavern Deluxe

Recognizing patterns in order to traverse a certain amount of distance is our core mechanism, so how do we support that? Well, we obviously need some "objects" that can form patterns. Maybe there are walls you see that have an arrangement of stones (similar to a Go board) that change each time you advance.

Maybe the player can move, slide, or otherwise manipulate these patterns? Well, we have to be careful with this, because this is something that could fight with our core mechanism if it's too heavy. Is it about simply recognizing patterns? Or is it about manipulating them?

If it's only about recognizing them and then making a turn, perhaps there's an overmap of some sort. The visible pattern is a bit like the grid of tiles in *Minesweeper*, giving deductive clues as to which direction you should go next. Perhaps there are numbers or symbols that show the number of "things" in the next room, and things could be positive (like treasure that scores points) or negative. Maybe there are also other cues—like two stones together on the X axis are always the same kind of thing—and there are a few tiles that you can see plainly.

Perhaps, with enough of these kinds of "clues" and a few rules for how these clues emerge, we could have the beginnings of a system that works; the arrangement of things in the game support the core mechanism of recognizing patterns. However, we may also run into trouble with this idea. If we have difficulty making it not *too* based on deduction, then there might be an issue where it's only a matter of finding out which moves it isn't, and choosing randomly between those remaining.

This might be solved by adding more supporting mechanisms, although if you find yourself having to add too much in the way of secondary or even tertiary supporting mechanisms, you might want to go back to the drawing board. Maybe it *is* about manipulating patterns—rotating them or removing some of them. Don't be afraid to start over.

Elevator Urchin Dive

Since the core mechanism is valuation of positions, perhaps we can have some real-time, simple way for players to show their level of investment in a given position. One way that quickly comes to mind would be the ability to "charge up." Maybe when you press a button, your character slows down to almost a crawl (staying in the same place), but as he charges, it's some kind of high-risk, high-reward type of interaction. So perhaps if you "score" any sea urchins while doing this, they score with a bonus, but if you get hit (or possibly if you fail to score any urchins, or both), you suffer a big penalty. Perhaps this penalty, and the bonus, can scale with how long you've been "charging."

Other supporting mechanisms might be some details as to how the sea urchins themselves work. Maybe sea urchins can be collected only when you're moving slowly—if you hit them at high speed, they knock you away. This supports the positioning aspect of the core mechanism in an obvious way, but is also a nice double-edged sword.

Fancy Portrait Trader

There's a number of directions we could go with this, but perhaps you have private cards that have different denominations of money on them. You could, perhaps, have a supporting "blind bid" mechanism where players play a bid face down on the table and simultaneously reveal, forcing players to guess at the valuation of the other players. Or staying with the bidding mechanism, perhaps it could be more direct, and players could take turns increasing a bid. Both of these might work as a primary supporting mechanism.

That might not be enough inherent complexity, however, to make the game interesting. Perhaps each player has a special "identity" card that's hidden, that only they can see. This identity card biases them towards certain paintings in a way that other players don't know about. Perhaps there is a point bonus at the end of the game for every "Red" painting you have. Players might start to pick up on this throughout the game and even try to use it against you. While we won't know until we test it, this might be a good supporting mechanism because of how it clearly supports the core mechanism.

SUPPORTING A PHANTOM CORE

This phase—selecting supporting mechanisms to try to adequately support your core—is one of the most difficult, arduous, and also the most fun parts of game design. Unless you get extremely lucky, 95% of the supporting mechanisms you propose for a system will fail once tested. However, by knowing about the clockwork design pattern, you can at least know where to look. Without this design pattern, you might be just adding new mechanisms arbitrarily, or because they "seem cool."

As a very clear example, maybe a person would add an "attack" action to *Fancy Portrait Trader*. For instance, let's say that players each have ten health, and when someone buys a portrait, players can attack him. He also has defense cards that can block some of the attacks. This might seem on paper to actually work, and it also might even seem like it works in testing!

However, ultimately, what you've done is create two distinct core mechanisms. Attacking them really has nothing to do with that original core mechanism. Even if it's technically "triggered by" the core mechanism, the difference is that it doesn't support it. This means that it's actually supporting something else, some other core mechanism that isn't even really there. This is something that you can see frequently if you look to AAA videogames, where the clockwork game design pattern is almost never found.

Worse yet is that sometimes designers will implement new goals to support their new accidental "secondary core mechanism." For instance, with the attack mechanism, it's rather natural to assume a rule like, "if you reach zero health, you have been eliminated and have lost the game" (indeed, the concept of "health" itself tends to suggest the goal of reducing it to zero).

Many have been tempted to think that having multiple unrelated goals going on at once in the same system is a good thing. This is because in a system that is very weak to begin with—which describes most games of any type—adding some noise such as multiple victory conditions can seem to make the game more interesting, in the short run.

In the long run, however, what always happens is that players figure out which of the two goals is actually the optimal one to go for, which is the easiest to achieve. This is a case of inherent imbalance and cannot be fixed with any amount of fine-tuning. There is always going to be one goal that makes the most sense.

Further, having two unrelated goals tends to cause games to have a kind of "random" or "chaotic" feeling to them. You are working within one game, trying to achieve one goal, and then another player, pursuing a different goal, does some actions that don't even use the language of the game you're playing. For instance: imagine that I'm trying to make a great bid, and then suddenly someone attacks me and kills me. I was thinking hard about the question of what would be a good bid to make, and suddenly I was killed via some other rule. In practice, many players would just find that an annoying delay in their pursuit of getting better at the bidding game.

To make it even clearer, why not play a match of chess wherein both players have to keep bouncing a balloon over their head. If either of them knock the balloon so far away from themselves that they can't reach it without getting up, they also lose the match of chess. Obviously the skill of bouncing the balloon over one's head has nothing to do with chess. Most players would rightly have a feeling of "can we just play chess, without the balloon aspect?" The balloon aspect clearly has nothing to do with the strategic game, and it's far less interesting.

Avoid having multiple goals in your games. Instead, put multiple constraints or conditions on one clear goal. So, the goal might be "destroy your opponent's units *and* buildings," or "destroy the opponent's units, buildings, and get his hand size down to three cards," or something. Of course, the more of these constraints you put on the game, the more messy it will be to learn and play, but it's still better than allowing players to have to somewhat arbitrarily choose goals while they play. Players should be focused entirely on choosing strategy, and not at all on choosing goals.

GOAL IS YOUR ANCHOR

Throughout the process of choosing supporting mechanisms, you should always keep the goal in mind. A way that you can think of your supporting mechanisms is that they lead to your goal, and that your goal is an "ultimate expression" of your core mechanism.

The ultimate expression of a core mechanism.

To take a couple of quick examples: in chess, the core mechanism is "positioning to take control," so it makes sense that you'd have one crucial piece that both players want to take control of. If you can take control of the enemy king, that's the ultimate expression of having taken control of the board, given that the other player knows all along that if you do that, you will win the game, so they're doing everything they can to make sure that this doesn't happen.

In *Super Smash Bros.*, the core mechanism is "attacking to knock the opponent back." So, knocking an opponent "back" so much that they leave the stage makes sense as a logical "ultimate goal" for that core mechanism.

EXERCISES

1. Create elevator pitches—quickly and without thinking much about it, jot down one to three sentences that give a basic elevator pitch for a new game idea. Don't worry about whether your game makes sense.
2. Wacky title card game—in quick succession, come up with five titles for card games that don't exist. Try to be strange and unusual—this will make the next exercise more interesting.
3. Analyze your pitches—take work from the previous two exercises and attempt to find a goal and supporting mechanisms.

Section 2 **ANALYSIS**

While ultimately all gameplay mechanisms will stand or fall in the testing phase, there are ways of organizing information that will help you identify bad ideas upfront, speeding up the overall development process and allowing your game to become a much better one in the time you have.

In the same way that it's helpful to put an idea into words on paper, in that it helps you to better understand your own idea, creating documents that explain the gameplay purpose of your game elements is extremely helpful.

CHARTS

The first method is making charts. Charts are probably the most useful tool that a designer has for helping him analyze his game elements. What we mean by a chart is a two-axis grid of information. So, along the far left column you might have a list of all the items in your game, and then in each row you have their damage rating, their armor rating, their weight, and their cost. This way, you can quantify values and possibly find problems before you even implement anything.

The big question with charts is, what are we going to chart? Chances are, a chart that displays all of the relevant information in your game is going to be so large as to be unreadable. As you'll see, designing a good chart is a discipline of its own, an inexact art form that requires a keen and careful sense of how to quantify value and keep complex concepts clear in your mind.

What really makes the charting process useful is the process of numeric valuation. For example, let's say you have three kinds of weapons in your game, and you want them all to have different, but balanced, qualities. You have swords, polearms, and crossbows. These items have three qualities, which we'll write out below.

Weapon	Damage	Range	Cost
Sword	25 points	1	$10
Polearm	15 points	4	$20
Crossbow	10 points	8	$40

Now, these are the actual numeric qualities of these items, but that's not what we actually care about. What's written here are the literal values, but what we want to know as designers are effective values. Just because the polearm has four times the range of the sword does not mean that the polearm's range is necessarily four times as good as that of the sword. There are many other factors that might weigh in. For example, what if the screen itself is only six of those units wide? In this case, it might be the case that many times your weapon's range is farther than you can even see, and therefore the utility of that range is diminished. The value of the eight-range crossbow on a six-wide screen would also be extremely deceptive!

Or take another example. The literal value cost of the polearm appears to be twice that of the sword, but that doesn't necessarily mean that the sword is "twice as good" when it comes to the matter of price. For instance, perhaps the distribution of money in your game is irregular. Maybe the first ten dollars are somewhat easy to find, but after that it gets harder. If this was the case, the seeming "twice as good" sword might be three or four times as good on the matter of price.

So this is why we try to abstract things into effective values. In a game where the first ten dollars are easier to find than additional dollars, the screen is six range units wide, and most units have 15 hit points, we might abstract out the values using a one to three star rating, with three stars being "good," two stars being "decent," and one star being "bad."

Weapon	Damage	Range	Cost
Sword	★ ★ ★	★	★ ★ ★
Polearm	★ ★ ★	★ ★ ★	★ ★
Crossbow	★	★ ★ ★	★

RELATIVE VALUES

Making a chart like this, the values are always relative. So, if two things have three stars, and then it's discovered that one of those things is actually much better than previously thought, you might express that by moving one of the two items down to a two-star rating.

Now, don't worry too much about the actual number of stars given in each column. It can be difficult to quantify such things, and it's mostly impossible in this situation where we're talking about a hypothetical game in such abstract terms. What's important is that you understand the concept.

The sword and the polearm both get three stars on damage, because both of them will instantly kill a bad guy outright in this game. The sword does not get extra stars for having more damage than the polearm, because that extra damage doesn't do anything more.

On range, the sword has bad range, and the other two have more range than you'd ever need, so they both get three stars. Again, the crossbow's extra range beyond that of the polearm doesn't help it much (if at all) because of how small the screen is. One thing to note, though, is that even if the crossbow's range does help it a little in this situation, it might not be significant enough to have it get an extra star. If it did help enough, then what you would likely do is move the polearm's effective value in this category to two stars.

For cost, the sword has the best cost, because it's easy to get that ten gold. If we know it's significantly harder to get the next ten gold to get the polearm, then it definitely must be much harder to get another 20 gold with which to purchase the crossbow. So, it should get a one-star rating, and the polearm gets two stars.

Again, don't get too hung up on whether or not you agree with these assessments—this is simply a demonstration of the technique itself. The final step is to add another column on the far right which gets the average number of stars, like this:

Weapon	Damage	Range	Cost	AVERAGE
Sword	★ ★ ★	★	★ ★ ★	2.3 stars
Polearm	★ ★ ★	★ ★ ★	★ ★	2.6 stars
Crossbow	★	★ ★ ★	★	1.6 stars

We've added up the number of total stars, which, if our assessments were correct, and if there are no other factors determining value, should be a decent indicator as to the actual effective value of these items. The conclusion is that, right now, the polearm is probably the best weapon, although only by a small margin over the sword.

Of course, in reality, you would almost never have such a simple chart. If a game's easy to chart, it's easy to solve. You should realize that in making these charts, you're doing exactly what a player will do in his mind when he tries to make optimal decisions. All we're doing is writing it down on paper, taking it seriously and hopefully doing it better than most of our players will. We then use this information to fine-tune our balance.

Here's an example of a slightly more realistic-looking chart.

Weapon	DMG	RNG	Cost	Time	Attack speed	Ease of use	Utility	AVERAGE
Sword	★ ★ ★	★	★ ★ ★	★ ★ ★	★ ★ ★	★ ★ ★	★ ★ ★	2.71
Polearm	★ ★ ★	★ ★ ★	★ ★	★ ★	★	★ ★	★	2.00
Crossbow	★	★ ★ ★	★	★	★	★ ★	★	1.42

You might notice that the totals have now shifted, with the sword now being significantly better than the polearm, despite what our other chart said. This is both a normal, expected part of the process, and also a cautionary sign: depending on how you design your chart, you can get wildly different results, so you must take extreme care.

When we start getting into detail like this, the real process of designing a good chart begins. There are a ton of difficult decisions that need to be made here in order for this chart to accurately depict the reality of your game. Let's quickly go over what these new qualities mean.

Time—this rating displays how quickly the user can access this item. Now, depending on how the game works, this may or may not be the same value as "cost." If you need to buy multiples of them throughout the game (perhaps for different party members, or if weapons sometimes break or are lost), then cost and time would definitely be separate values. Without such a thing, it might still be of value, but it might have diminished value, which we'll get into later.

Attack speed—this quantifies the amount of time it takes for your character to use the weapon. If it's slower, it means that it requires more prediction and is less forgiving, which would be a bad quality. Actually, we could split those into their own columns: a "warm-up" column, and a "cool-down" column—warm-up being the time between when you make the input and when it happens, and cool-down being the time between when the action happens and when you're allowed to make another input. We'll talk about this more in a bit.

Ease of use—this might be very difficult to quantify, and actually might be, at least partially, already expressed by the "attack speed" column. However, let's say that the weapons all fire in a different way—the sword is in a big arc in front of you, the polearm is in a diagonal upward jab, and the crossbow shoots with a curved downward arc. Probably, the sword will be the easiest to use because its attack zone is the least complicated; it's just your own hitbox, enlarged.

Utility—perhaps, in this game, the sword has a special feature, which is that it can also open treasure chests, while the other two weapons can't (normally, you have to jump on top of them). If that's the case, then this should probably be reflected in the final tally.

AVOIDING INFLATION

With the last example, you might be asking whether or not the utility of being able to open treasure chests is really worth three stars or not in that game. Another way to ask this question is: is the ability to open a treasure chest as significant as the cost, damage, or ease of use?

For the sake of discussion, let's say that it actually isn't as significant. Whether or not your weapon can open treasure chests is of less importance than whether it's easy to use or whether you can afford it. So, in fact, perhaps that shouldn't even get a column?

Then again, being able to open treasure chests is worth something, so not having it reflected in this chart would be inaccurate. There are a few ways to deal with this problem.

One way is to simply put a cap on how many stars a column can produce. So, even if relatively speaking, some things should have three stars and some should have two, we'd reduce any threes to twos. Of course, in this situation we are still losing information—our threes provide more utility than our twos.

A much more complicated and difficult to set up, but potentially more effective way, is to add weights to each column. So, let's say that there's a normal weight of five for each column. Columns that are slightly less important overall get a weight of three or four, and columns that are more important get a weight of six or seven. Weight is the number of times that this value is entered into the average.

So if something has a three-star rating in utility, but utility has a weight of only two, that means that the three-star rating is only going in twice, whereas most stats are going in five times. Here's a new chart, with weights added in parenthesis:

Weapon	DMG (6)	RNG (5)	Cost (5)	Time (5)	Attack Speed (3)	Ease of Use (3)	Utility (3)	AVERAGE
Sword	★★★	★	★★★	★★★	★★★	★★★	★★★	2.66
Polearm	★★★	★★★	★★	★★	★	★★	★	2.16
Crossbow	★	★★★	★	★	★	★★	★	1.43

You might notice that both attack speed and ease of use were reduced to three. This was because of the aforementioned potential redundancy between these qualities. You might instead have attack speed at four and reduce ease of use to two, or even keep ease of use at three. This is one of those small decisions that make the process of building a chart difficult.

SPREADSHEET GAMES

There are many systems— particularly D&D-inspired systems such as RPGs for example—that are really nothing but the numbers in a spreadsheet. While we use this technique to help us understand our systems in a somewhat quantifiable way, be wary of a system that is too quantifiable. If you can literally just add up numbers and do simple math to figure out when something's imbalanced, that means there's a problem—your system isn't providing enough emergent complexity.

So for the first row, we add up the values. The DMG for the sword is three, but we actually have six entries of that, so it's really going to add 18 points to our pre-average sum. We add up each box in this row in this way and have a pre-average sum of 80. Then, we divide that, not by the number of columns as before, but by the number of total weight (6+5+5+5+3+3+3 = 30) and we divide 80 by that number, which gives us 2.66.

We now have a knob we can turn that gives us control over how important certain qualities are. You can make this process even easier by using a program like Microsoft Excel or Google Spreadsheets. In programs such as these, it's possible to insert equations into cells so that they automatically update to the correct information anytime you change any numbers. I highly recommend that any game designer learn the basics of how to use a spreadsheet program for this reason.

MAPPING

Mapping is similar to creating charts, but helps to create a more visual representation of variables. For example, a basic but important map is one that we've discussed numerous times throughout this book—the "supporting mechanisms, core mechanisms, goal" map. It's highly recommended that you take the time to create one of these for every game that you make.

Sometimes, after making a basic game structure map, you may find that there are two or more significant supporting mechanisms that seem to need all of their own supporting mechanisms. Often, this signifies that one of those supporting mechanisms (or more) is actually fighting with

The basic game structure map

your core. This is especially true if the supporting mechanism itself has numerous supporting mechanisms that don't connect back to the core. In other words, if a supporting mechanism has a large number of its own supporting mechanisms that aren't shared by the core, then chances are you have a system with conflicting cores, and this needs to be resolved. Figure out a way to reconnect those secondary supporting mechanisms to the core, remove some of them, or even consider removing the large supporting mechanism itself.

In the following example, there are a number of serious problems. First off, it is unclear what the core mechanism for the game is supposed to be. By default, one might guess A since it's in the middle and has the most connections to the other major hubs, but it's unclear, and this will have a negative impact on the player's ability to understand the game.

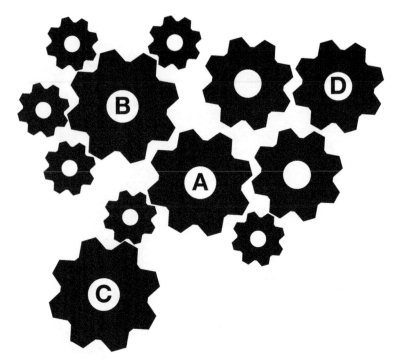

Numerous hierarchical problems.

MECHANISM HIERARCHY

A good general rule to follow is this: the complexity/weight/number of connections of a mechanism should never be greater than the mechanism above it. So, a tertiary supporting mechanism should never be larger or more complex than the secondary mechanism it's attached to and, of course, a secondary mechanism should never fight for dominance with the core. Complexity should descend as you move away from the core.

The problem with B is that it has a huge number of "unique connections"—tertiary (we assume?) mechanisms that connect to nothing else. This is highly inefficient. Each mechanism should be doing at least two jobs if possible. Having a single "one-job" mechanism can be OK, but a situation like this displays an egregious disregard for efficiency.

The problem with C and D are the same—they don't follow the rule of mechanism hierarchy. C is way heavier than the mechanism that it connects from, which will be confusing and strange to players. D isn't quite as bad, and may even be OK in some circumstances, but it's something to be wary of, for the same reason.

The supporting mechanisms aspect of it can get very detailed and complex. In fact, you'll sometimes want to have a chart that only focuses on supporting mechanisms, or even a specific type of supporting mechanism. For example, if your game has a bunch of different monsters, and you want to make sure that they all interact with each other in some way (as to create synergy), you might make a connections map of the monsters.

Connections maps show a detailed view of exactly how two game elements interact with each other. Generally speaking, in an elegant game, most individual elements will have a large number of connections relative to the number of elements in the game. This is because an elegant game does a lot with a little, and these connections are the very connections that make a game have deep emergent complexity.

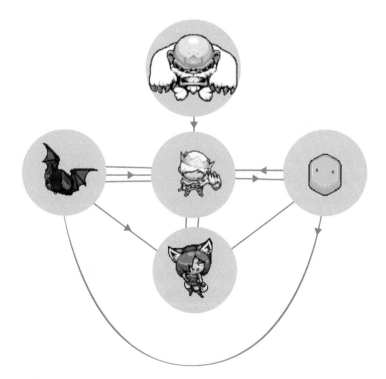

A connections map.

If, after making a connections map, you observe that there are significant mechanisms that do not feed back into each other very much, you may have a situation where your system's core is unclear. If this is the case, you should strongly consider creating more connections between the two large mechanisms, or removing one completely. In the latter case, you'll almost always need to bulk up the new core with some more depth.

Have you ever played a game that, when you thought about it, was really just a loosely connected series of minigames? Many videogames are this way—perhaps *Grand Theft Auto* or even the more recent *Legend of Zelda* games would be examples. What always happens in them is that one of those minigames is always most significant and interesting, and none of them are actually very deep.

In conclusion, whether you use charts, mapping, or any other kind of layout, what you should be doing is constantly analyzing the nature of your system. Preferably, you should be using both these systems, and also creating your own. In fact, a specific design may need its own form of lens in order to be adequately analyzed. Take your time on this problem and figure out a way to ask the right questions of your system—it will save you a hundred times the work down the line.

EXERCISES

1. Charting—find a game that already exists, and build a chart for it. Make a chart that lays out all of the characters/spells/abilities on the far left column, and a list of strategy-related properties on the top row. Then fill it out. Find another player of the game and see if they agree.

2. Mapping—create a "map" for that same game, and visually lay out the core mechanism, the goal, and any and all supporting mechanisms. Try to find a new way, not listed in this book, to portray the significance of these.

3. Analysis—analyze your charts and maps and see if there are any rule changes you could prescribe that would make that game better. Consult with others to see if they agree with the premises of your chart, and whether they agree with your solutions.

Section 3 **IMPLEMENTATION**

The previous parts of this chapter lay out the ways of thinking about your design holistically. As it was mentioned in the introduction to this book, this is not a book about programming or hands-on technical advice; however, in this section, some useful and practice information will be given on the topic of practical implementation advice for game designers, specifically. In other words, the above section is about how a game designer should *think*. This section is about what a game designer should *do*.

RESEARCH

Regardless of what your craft is, research is always incredibly important. In order to say something useful to people, you must be aware of what has already been said. Remember that you are adding your voice to a global conversation that has been going on for a long time.

So, you have to do a lot of research. Luckily for game designers, research often means playing games. In general, as a designer, you want to play as many games of as many different kinds as you can, for every one of those games gives you a new tool that you can work with and use in your designs.

Further, don't just play them—analyze them. Compare them with similar games from other mediums. How did they fail? How did they succeed? How could they be made better?

When designing a specific game, you're going to want to do more specific research. Use whatever classifications you can—genre, core mechanism, theme, or other criteria—and find out what has already been done.

For instance, let's say you want to make a two-player war-game. The first thing you might do is a simple search for "war-games" on the internet. You're likely to find a ton of stuff this way, but you might stumble on the "hex and counter" tabletop war-game genre. Dive into this genre. See if you can play some of the games that are considered the best in the genre. See if you can find some random obscure entries in the genre, too.

Or look to your core mechanism. Maybe it's "area control." If so, you can look to abstract board games for inspiration. Classics such as Go or chess, of course, but also the more recent Project GIPF games or others. Perhaps you can even look to modern digital war-games like *StarCraft* or *Dawn of War* for other ideas.

The point is, leave no stone unturned. If you are creating an area control war-game, then you need to be doing something with that that hasn't been done before. You need to solve problems that so far haven't been solved. Maybe, in your research, war-games all generally tend to have a "turtling" problem, where players play too defensively. You need to figure out how people have tried to solve that problem in the past and how and why their attempts failed.

Of course, if your game concept is totally novel, then you perhaps don't have to do as much research. However, you'd have to have done a ton of research in order to know that your game concept is novel so, either way, research is required. Further, a person with a limited background is highly unlikely to be capable of creating something novel in the first place.

Once you're a total expert on the kind of game you're intending to make, you can move onto the next step.

THE DESIGN DOCUMENT

The design document should start with a single sentence, and ultimately be a complete description of every mechanism in your game.

The first sentence you write should be like a "mission statement"— quite similar to the elevator pitch we discussed at the beginning of the chapter, but with more of a focus on what it is you are trying to do here. For instance: "Create a multiplayer fighting game that's all about deflection." Put it in bold and leave it at the top of your document. That way, you can always refer back to that original mission statement and see if you're getting off track, or if you want to revise your mission statement.

There are many ways to write a design document, and you should experiment and find one that works well for you. One very useful way, however, is to write the design document as though it is a rulebook or manual that players must read.

Basically, imagine that you're going to give this rulebook over to some players, along with any necessary components, and the players should be able to actually play your game with nothing but that. They can't ask you any questions; all questions must be answered in the document.

Often, a good way to organize a design document is something like this:

1. Introduction/purpose statement
2. Gameplay overview—a quick rundown on the sorts of things that players will be doing, and what the goal of the game is.

   a. Number of players
   b. List of components
   c. Suggested ages

3. Starting the game—a list of steps that players must do at the start of the game. For example, selecting a character, drawing cards, or any other compulsory tasks.
4. How to play—this actually instructs players on what inputs they can, or must, make. For turn-based games, this can often be a list of "phases," like action phase, draw phase, resolution phase, for example. For real-time games, it will be more of a general description of the actions available and any time or other constraints.
5. Game elements—this describes each type of action. In this section, other mechanisms will be listed, such as "special actions" or something involving resources. These other details will be explained, one by one—what kinds of actions are there? What kinds of limitations are there? Are there maps? Basically, this section should really lay out, in general, what the basic kinds of elements of the game are— the next section will list the elements/components themselves.
6. Elements in detail—this will be the biggest section, page-wise, of the entire document. This actually will list individual game components. For instance, if you were designing *Super Smash Bros.*, you might list the characters here in detail, listing all of their moves and exactly what they do. You would also list the different gameplay modes, stages, items, and any other specific gameplay elements.

7. Game end—if you choose, this section can go either at the beginning or end of your document. Either way, this should very clearly describe the game-end conditions in great detail. What is the game-end condition? What is the win-condition? Are there any tie-breaking rules?

8. FAQ/other notes—optional. Sometimes, it's good to provide an FAQ (frequently asked questions) section that fills in a few exceptions and details that other areas of the document didn't cover. For example, you might think of a few strange "edge-case" scenarios. For instance, if it's *Super Smash Bros.*, you might have a question that reads, "what happens if a player tries to grab an edge, but there's already another player holding onto that edge?"—as well as your answer to that question, of course.

9. Strategy—optional. This can be difficult, but a lot of times it's an excellent exercise to help you imagine your game in action. If you have to think of and write down some basic strategy advice for your game, often the process of doing that will illuminate possible problems or weakness in your design.

You may want to use wiki software for your design document. Wikis are online, so it's easy for other team members to read your work, and anyone (or just certain people that you specify) can edit them. This makes them great for collaborations. Further, wikis are generally organized into pages that can interlink to each other in a non-linear way. This is especially good for game design documents since game design documents, like the game designs they describe, are non-linear. This makes writing, or reading, a linear game design document quite difficult. Ask anyone who has learned a European designer board game from reading the rules—it can be confusing.

PROTOTYPING

Every existing book on game design or game development talks about the necessity of prototyping. It's universally agreed that the more prototyping you are able to do before you start actually implementing things into your final work, the better off your final work will be.

This is because, despite the fact that building charts, graphs, design documents, or other materials can help you figure out what your game should be like, ultimately the thing that will really show you is when you actually put it into action.

Depending on the kind of game you're making, the nature of prototype implementation can vary wildly. Here are a few bits of advice for making a few common types of games.

Card Games

If you're making a game that involves cards, the cheapest way to make a prototype is to use (if possible) a standard deck of playing cards. Then, create a cheat sheet (or several sheets if it's a multiplayer game) that tells you what each card represents. So something like, "Jack = attack card, hearts = health potions," etc.

Another way to do card game prototypes is a bit more involved, but way easier to work with once you've done some work up front. This method involves designing some very rough cards on the computer using any kind of digital image editing/painting software (Photoshop probably being the best-known example) and then printing them out. You can buy card stock cheaply, but it's probably cheaper in the long run to buy card sleeves. If you put a real card (perhaps from an old Magic: The Gathering or Trivial Pursuit deck; many people have these lying around somewhere in the house) in there with your printed paper card, it feels and acts quite like a real card.

Turn-Based Tactical Games

Whether your tactical game will ultimately be physical or digital, you should be able to make a rough mockup of it using just a paper, pencil, and some tokens (coins or action figures or whatever's handy). It might require a lot of bookkeeping, but remember: any rules that are too much for the player to remember are also too much for the player to factor into strategy. Rules like these should almost certainly be disposed of, and creating a physical prototype is a great way to fish those kinds of rules out.

Digital Games

Unless you're a programmer yourself, prototyping a game that fundamentally must be digital (for instance, most real-time games) will be very difficult. However, there is a growing number of "game maker" -type programs that can help. This kind of software will usually have a somewhat user-friendly front-end that makes it relatively easy for a non-programmer to build a game. You'll definitely have to do some tutorials and read some documentation, but learning to use software like this is definitely worth all the effort, and it's still significantly easier than learning to program.

However, learning to program should also not be off the table. There are more and more free resources online that can teach you how to code and, beyond just game design, it's a great skill to have. Game designers usually need many skills, but if they could only have one, programming might be a contender for that position. Being able to get in there and change things yourself makes the iteration loop way faster, which ultimately means a better game in the same amount of time.

Finally, if you have a budget, it's definitely worth paying a programmer to program and maintain a prototype. This is a step that many established teams skip, unfortunately. If you have to, it's certainly worth taking something like 25–30% out of your art/music budget and putting that into a prototyping/pre-visualization phase. Nothing is more important than your game actually being mechanically good in the first place.

PLAYTESTING

Playtesting is the process of playing a game for the purposes of discovering design problems, bugs, or any other issues.

Once you have a prototype built, it's time to playtest. Playtesting is generally not as fun as the word might suggest, although there are definitely exciting moments. Unless you have a budget for paying your playtesters, you'll often have to ask friends or strangers to come try out your game. This is much more difficult than it sounds, because actually, being a playtester is somewhat difficult. You have to constantly learn new rules and then try to get invested in a game whose rules you know could (and likely will) change another 100 times before its release (if it ever even gets released). In addition to this, most prototypes are simply awful, don't work, fall flat, are too long, too short, unfair, tedious, clunky or otherwise offensive in some way. It takes a lot of patience to be a playtester.

So you're in the awkward position of having to ask people to be in that position, over and over and over again. If you're making a single-player game, you can heap some of the playtesting on yourself, although a designer playtesting his own game is of limited value. Sure, you'll be able to fix some obvious low-hanging-fruit problems, but there is so much that won't occur to you, since you're the person who actually wrote these rules. Worse, there's so much that did occur to you, that would never occur to another player when they sit down to play your game. So, something that you thought was obvious is actually anything but, and the only way to fish these things out is by having other people playtest your game—a lot.

The more playtesters the better, although in general you're in a good place if you have at least three to five serious playtesters. Serious play-testers are people who play the game every day, or almost every day, and interact with you every time they play. These people often should ulti-mately be getting game design credits themselves—they tend to submit hundreds of new ideas, many of which are good enough to get used in your final version.

In fact, once you have a good amount of playtesters, your role as designer starts to become less of a "rule generator" and more of a "system curator." Your job becomes mostly approving or not approving of ideas that other people come up with. Everyone can come up with ideas, after all, but you're the one with the good, developed sense for system design that will be able to ultimately make the call as to whether Good Idea #146 should be in this game or not (using many of the tools described in this book, hopefully).

It's recommended that you create some kind of space for playtesting. If it's a physical game that you play with others, schedule some days and times for playtesting to happen, or else it's likely not to happen. Either way, you should also consider creating some free internet forums as a place for you, your testers, and others to debate the pros and cons of various new design possibilities.

Sometimes it's best to be a third party while your game is being play-tested, rather than be a player yourself. It can be difficult to worry about making the best moves in your game while at the same time struggling to make sure that the game is working. For example, as the designer, you might forego a particularly powerful option because of your own fear that choosing it might flatten the possibility space. You should generally have other players play your game, and tell them to play seriously. Then, you should simply observe what happens and take notes.

ITERATION

Generally speaking, iteration means "making a new version" in response to feedback from testers. Of course, this feedback should have been processed by you already, as the design curator. Here's how the loop works best:

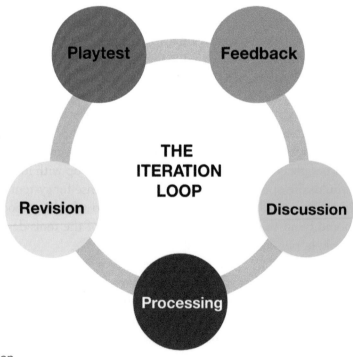

The loop

- Playtest—as we already discussed, playtesting is playing the game and/or observing it being played.
- Feedback—discuss the game with the playtesters and get their reactions. Generally it's a good idea to write down almost every significant note that anyone had about your game in this phase, as well as your own immediate observations.
- Discussion—after playing and getting initial feedback, press further. Ask general questions like "did it feel balanced?", "did it feel like you had options?", "did you feel overwhelmed?", or even possibly "was it fun?" Also ask for suggestions—"should we make this stronger?" or "should we add another supporting mechanism?" Forums are a great place to do this.
- Processing—review your own observations, as well as the discussion. This is the time to make charts, and constantly check everything against your core mechanism and your statement of purpose. Eventually, make some decisions for the next version.
- Revision—implement the changes you decided upon in the last step, and prepare a new version for testing, and the loop begins again.

DESIGN PHASE PITFALLS

There are a number of very common pitfalls that you should be aware of while building your game.

Feature Creep

Feature creep is the problem of incremental "bloating" of your game. One by one, more and more features are continually getting added to your game until there's just way too much. This is a widely known problem, although if you are following the design pattern as described in this book, there will be less temptation generally to allow it to happen. It is actually more of a temptation to add more noise to a generally noisy design. If playtesters see that your game is tight and clean, there will be a lot less clamoring for noisy, out-of-place elements (since they simply stand out so much in such a context).

Married to Previous Design Decisions

Be wary of getting too tied down by early numeric decisions you make. For instance, if you decided that there are 15 weapons in your game, don't feel stuck to that. Maybe there are 20 weapons, and maybe there are only four. Maybe there is only one!

Nice Round Numbers

Also be wary of numbers that are "nice and round," like 100 or 20. Chances are, if you're really balancing carefully and finding the right number that's balanced in your system, you aren't going to end up with nice neat round numbers like that. Of course, it's possible that you would—round numbers are still just numbers, after all—but there are a suspicious amount of round numbers in videogames.

Listening Too Much

Of course, this can be a problem on both sides. It's quite difficult to know when to listen to your playtesters' concern, and when to ignore them. However, one thing to remember is that, ultimately, *you* are the keeper of this design document, and whether it succeeds or fails is *your* responsibility. So, while you should give serious consideration to the concerns of playtesters, ultimately you need to decide for yourself. Beyond simply not being game designers themselves (usually), playtesters have a number of significant limitations. One such limitation is our next point.

Local Maxima

Sometimes, you'll be working on a game, and things will seem to be working. Things may even stay at this point of working pretty well, and you and the testers get rather used to it. But then someone, most often you, imagines a different way that it could be, and that way could potentially be much better. So you try it and, actually, it's worse. Now, the logical thing to do is to revert to before you made that latest change, right?

Well . . . maybe. Sometimes, a game has to become worse before it gets better. It can be difficult to know if the new change was actually a bad idea, or if the idea just needs more time to mature.

Playtesters very frequently fall into the local maxima trap. They get very attached to things as they are, and they might have a hard time understanding some dramatic change you have in mind. They will often take the failure of the first version of your new idea as proof that their skepticism was well-placed.

Of course, sometimes they're right. So you do have to be receptive, but just be aware that people sometimes get attached to things the way they are.

Losing the Core

Designing a good strategy game can take years, and, over the course of development, it's possible to get a bit sidetracked. Some games have many different modes, maps, characters, or even different "screens," and sometimes one of these elements can become a "game of its own." As we discussed in the previous chapter, if a game has more than one "core," it's going to cause all kinds of problems, so make sure that this doesn't end up happening by accident. Separate "screens" tend to threaten to do this often.

Changing Several Things at Once

When you're trying to identify an imbalance or other gameplay problem, it's often good to change just one element of the game at a time, so that you can see what effect that singular mechanism is having. If you change several large gameplay elements at once, you may have a difficult time interpreting feedback.

Rushing It

It should go without saying that you should take your time. Great games are complex, and it takes time for weaknesses to show themselves sometime. You may think after a week of testing that everything seems fine, only to find a month later that there is some really imbalanced element. Keep in mind that your game should ideally withstand competitive play for years. You can patch it, of course, but you want players to get the sense that you care about the solidness of your game early on.

POST-RELEASE

A game is not "done" once you release it. Really, there should never be a point where a game is "done"; if anything, a game should only ever be "done, for now."

We live in a world of practical limitations—limitations of time, of money, or even of motivation—and so sometimes those limitations get between us and continuing to work on a game. If that happens, there's not a lot that can be done about it.

However, whenever it's possible, we should always continue to improve our game. When you or the community playing the game identifies a problem, if you can, you really owe it to that community to fix it.

Thus, "release day" is a somewhat arbitrary point in a game's life, that's essentially "the point in development where the developer feels confident enough in it that he's ready to expose the world to it." By no means should anyone think of "release day" as the day you are "done" with the game. Release day is, in a sense, just the beginning for a game, because that's when your game is really tested for the first time. Even if you have highly active, responsive and smart beta testers—even if you have hundreds of them, working for years—the efforts they apply to finding faults in your game is a drop in the bucket compared to the first six months of being exposed to thousands or millions of players.

Beyond the fact that you should be continuing to work on your game post-release whenever possible, the way you should process and iterate on feedback is largely the same as it would be before release.

CHAPTER **4**

PITFALLS

The previous chapters have been a constructive, step-by-step walk through of the theory and application of the clockwork design pattern. In this chapter, we will go through some of the many pitfalls that designers should be aware of when building a game; common design practices that tend to hurt rather than help a designer create a great strategy game. Later in the chapter, I will also discuss my personal experiences with some of the games I've worked on in the past, and provide insight into some of the pitfalls I experienced on those projects.

By no means is this a complete list of potential problems, but these are some of the most common issues. Some of these problems might intuitively seem to be good qualities at first glance, and are considered par for the course in game design today.

It's also difficult to identify some of these issues because of the fact that they are so common. Some of these qualities can even be found in many popular, well-liked games. However, it should be remembered that just because something is well-liked, does not mean that we can't do far better in the future.

Section 1 **PROBLEMS**

DECEIVING THE PLAYER

If one is trying to build a strong contest of decision-making, there are some common qualities that we should be wary of. This is not to say, "never use these properties in your game at all," but simply a warning that heavy use of them will be damaging to your system as a contest of decision-making.

The reason anyone uses any of these properties in the first place is generally because they are quick and easy ways to avoid solvability. However, the extension is illusory, because the game is actually highly solvable, but some unrelated obstacle has been put in the way to stop the solution process (or execution of the solution). In this way, you've now built a system that lives or dies based on its success in deceiving the player.

Note that these are properties that designers actively put into their game; they are not usually a result of an accident. For contrast, a game being imbalanced is certainly an issue that would diminish the quality of a contest of decision-making; however, no one ever intentionally puts imbalance into their games. It is well-understood that imbalance is bad and we do what we can to minimize it. So if there is imbalance in our games, it's by accident, whereas the following qualities are things that designers intentionally put into their games.

Labor/Chores

Labor is, roughly, a task that takes some amount of time, but absolutely no thought. Labor is simply something you have to "do." For example, if a game asks you to run down a corridor, or bring an item to a position—these kinds of tasks are often simple rote "chores," and not really part of the greater strategy game. In a way, any "solved" part of your game could be called "labor," but you

can't always help it when your game gets solved. You can help the fact that you made your map so huge that walking across it is laborious.

This is an incredibly common property in many digital games, which are often highly concerned with the idea of fantasy simulation. Real life contains constant instances that we might call labor. If you want to get a donut out of the fridge, that means you have to walk over to the refrigerator, which is purely labor; no decisions need to be made, and it's not even a matter of execution. You basically have zero chances of failing, and it's not as though there is some other, potentially better way of getting the donut.

Why does labor ever appear in games? We play games to have fun, so what kind of a designer would ever intentionally put labor into their games? Well, not all designers are aware of when they're putting labor into their games, as is the case with, for example, some first-person shooter combat games that have huge maps. It's not always clear to these designers that this means that players are going to be doing a lot of "walking to the refrigerator." If the map is sufficiently large, however, there's bound to be a lot of labor.

But the other reason is that labor plays an interesting trick on us. Everyone has played the board game Monopoly, usually with house rules that make the game (not a great game to begin with) far worse. For instance, many people play Monopoly without bidding for properties. When played this way, there are essentially no decisions to make in the game, other than possibly "should I buy this property I just landed on," which is mostly solved. Yet, people have been playing Monopoly in that way for years. If they have essentially no decisions to make, then shouldn't they be getting more bored with it more quickly?

One answer is actually the way money works in the game. Prices for properties generally are non-rounded amounts like $142, yet the bills in the game are all normal money denominations of $1, $5, $10, $20, $50 and so on. What this means is that any time a money transaction has to happen—which is almost every turn—players have to "break bills" and "get change." The combination of the light arithmetic that needs to be done to do that and the physical activity of breaking bills creates an illusion of "doing something." It's just enough to occupy most adult's brains to keep them from remembering that they have no decisions to make.

The reality is that designers consciously and unconsciously use this same technique to distract players from other similarly-solved systems. In many RPGs, what you have to *do* is obvious and solved—bring this item to that point on the map—but in order to do it you have to walk all that way. Not only that, but along the way you have to fight random encounter battles, each of which are also totally solved, but have just enough "bill-breaking" type activity for you to do to keep your brain occupied.

As an example, the combat in a game like *Final Fantasy* is quite similar to the task of breaking bills. A character with a powerful attack is kind of like a large bill—you have to make sure to put it in the right spot. A character with a lighter attack is kind of like a $10 added onto a $100 to meet the $110 price.

Of course, using labor in this way actually solves nothing. All it does is distract people from the fact that they're interacting with a solved system. Instead, the solution is to make interesting and unsolved systems.

An interesting thing to note is that if you do have an unsolved and interesting system, players will actually notice labor much more, because now it's no longer "something to do while I wait for something interesting to happen." It has now interrupted the interesting thing I was doing.

Is there any place for labor in good strategy games? Of course. Arguably, even moving a chess piece is a bit of labor. Also it's almost certain that some aspects of your game will be solved (often times, the very end game or very early game, for example), and in these cases, the player is arguably engaging in "labor." So, it's OK if your system isn't 100% labor-free. The objective is to minimize it, and certainly not add in anything that adds unnecessary labor.

Execution

Inspired by sports, videogames (particularly those played in real-time) tend to embrace a certain degree of execution skill. In the same way that a skilled American football quarterback is able to aim his throw to complete a pass play, a 2D fighting

game player might execute a long and difficult combo that involves a long string of precisely-timed button presses.

We, as a civilization have had great appreciation for the ability to "execute something well," going back to ancient times. However, it should be very clear to game designers that "someone's ability to execute an action" is a very different matter from "whether or not that person should execution the action." To put it succinctly, "can" is separate from "should."

Games, as described in this book, are systems of "should." Should I move this piece here? Should I advance on the enemy when he approaches? Should I build this kind of unit? Should I cash in now? As we've discussed already, it's a matter of making a decision, not simply finding out if you *can* do a certain action.

In the many pre-design eras that came before our time, there were not many "well-designed games." One quick and simple way to make a solved system seem unsolved and potentially interesting is to add execution to it.

For example, take the game of Tic-Tac-Toe. It's solved, and therefore uninteresting. However, let's make the following modifications to Tic-Tac-Toe: you now draw the board about six feet wide in sand. Then, you must stand 20 feet away and throw spears at the board (with little X and O flags hanging off the ends) to make your moves.

Now, suddenly, Tic-Tac-Toe seems a little bit more interesting, and one could picture adults engaging with such a system, at least in a social, light, fun way. Double or triple the distance, and we might suddenly be looking at an "Olympic sport," played competitively and taken very seriously, because of the physical prowess now required.

We've now added some basic execution to the system, causing players to "mess up" sometimes and make an input that they didn't mean to make. Take a common Tic-Tac-Toe example, where one player has the game locked down, and it is his turn.

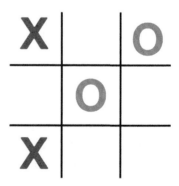

X player has the game . . . or does he?

Without the element of execution (or some other type of variance), it's simply a done-deal. The X player will complete his three in a row, and the game is over. But with the execution, we now add the chance that the X player will simply "mess up" his execution, and the O player will get another chance. So now it seems like "who knows—anyone could win!" A kind of ambiguity is indeed there.

Street Fighter and other 2D fighting games are well known for their intentional injection of execution into the system to create exactly this kind of ambiguity. Many moves have difficult-to-input motions, such as the famous dragon punch, or Zangief's spinning piledriver. The thinking was—and still is—if you make those moves simple to execute, the game will be solved, or mostly solved. In order for the game to work at most levels of play, it requires the possibility of players "messing up" and not doing the thing they intended to do.

Such a "mess up" actually creates a confusing bit of noise in the system. You may have chosen a great move for the situation, but simply failed to execute it, and ultimately end up losing. As we discussed, the win/loss state informs the meaning of every move that came before it, so what the player ends up getting is a somewhat "dishonest" game— a game for which the feedback can't really be trusted. Were the moves that the player intended to make good moves?

Over a long enough period of time, players play enough games where they can start to "tune out the noise" and eventually average out the noisy results into meaningful feedback, but it's far from optimal to force players to do this. Effectively, by introducing execution elements, you're introducing "execution luck."

Almost any game played in real time (continuous time) is going to have some degree of an execution element to it, so, as with labor, this isn't something we can entirely get rid of. As with labor, the objective is to minimize it, and certainly not to add things like complicated inputs designed to cause input errors.

If one wanted to create a system that "measures a person's ability to make correct inputs," contests are the place to do that. For games, we're measuring a player's decision-making, so execution tends to get in the way of that.

Memorization

A single-player game must have randomness/procedurally generated content in order to function as a game. Without this, players simply memorize the moves that worked last time and they will work every time. Once the player has won a match once, he can now win every single time, so long as he's able to remember all of the inputs he made last time.

In this way, memorization can be a thing that takes over the role that decision-making would have had to fill otherwise.

Memorization also manifests in terms of games that have extremely high levels of inherent complexity. Some games are so complex that a big part of the "skill" of the game is just knowing what all of the things do. The famous Rogue-like game *Nethack* might be one of the best examples of this. There are such an incredible wealth of *things* in the game—in fact, the game even has a "kitchen sink" in it—which highlights the designer's desire to make the amount of rules in the game a novelty feature (even more crazy is how many rules there are attached to the sink item in the game!). A colleague of mine once referred to this type of design as "wiki design," because it "basically requires you to open a wiki while playing."

In a game such as this, a huge chunk of "getting good at it" simply means memorizing a vast array of information. Knowledge of this kind certainly is a skill, but if the game is

MEMORIZED OPENINGS

Many deterministic games will have "memorized openings" that must be learned to play at a competitive level. Some games even have end-games that must similarly be memorized. While this is a bad thing that should be minimized as much as possible, keep in mind that it's impossible to have a deterministic game without memorized openings. You can avoid having memorized openings only by introducing random events or hidden information, but if you're modifying your system in this way just to avoid memorized openings, you may be throwing the baby out with the bathwater.

really just a "measure what percentage of the knowledge the user knows," then it's really a contest, not a game.

Of course, all games require some memorization. Rules themselves must be memorized, and even strategy is of course memorized to some degree. However, in a well-designed game, memory's role in strategy will be to remember tiny situations that just help color your decision-making process, not dominate it. A "memorized opening," for instance, in chess would be an example of memory dominating strategy. Multiple moves take place wherein the player is making no choices, only following a list of prescribed commands. Instead, having a loose heuristic model that says "in general when someone does this, you might want to do that" is what we want. In other words: keep the bits of useful memory as small and as loose as possible.

Output Randomness

As we've discussed, a game system is a causal chain—or web—of events: this happened, therefore this player made this decision, therefore that happened. A chain of logical, rational events happen, leading to an outcome (win/loss), and from that win/loss you can trace the logic all the way back to the start of the game. From this process, you can gain understanding.

Some games, however, interject things like "dice rolls" or other bits of variance into the play. So, you might make a great move—the optimal move, even—but the dice rolls poorly, and now you're in a bad position, despite having made a great move. This kind of randomness I refer to as "output randomness."

On the other hand, some games have random effects that occur in the game, which don't immediately affect the player.

While input randomness is randomness that informs your decision—such as a random map layout or random market cards that are drawn—*output* randomness determines the *outcome* of your decision. There are some grey areas between the two, but it's a very important distinction to be made.

The main difference is the distance between when the information becomes public, and when it actually causes an impact on the player. In general, you should always try to make sure that these two things do not happen at the same time. Think of the classic war game "fog of war" technique. That's normally "input randomness"—you can see enemy units a few tiles away, and you have some time to take the knowledge of their existence into account. Now imagine if you could only see what's in a tile if you actually enter the tile itself—that's what output randomness is like!

Just as execution can often cause a game system to need to be played many, many times before "honest feedback" is received by the player, output randomness delivers noisy outcomes that cannot be understood.

For example, take the famous board game Risk. You decide to attack a certain area of the map. Is that a good move or a bad move? Surely the game will give us feedback for this, if not right away, at least by the end of the game. Well, what actually happens is a random outcome.

WHAT IS "RANDOM?"

When should we consider something "random," exactly? Obviously, things like dice rolls and card draws are designed to be random, as in "unpredictable." They're designed to be a thing that players don't ever learn to predict. There are other things which are similarly random—for instance, simultaneous action, as in Rock-Paper-Scissors. While some players can potentially guess correctly a higher percentage of the time than others, ultimately the simultaneous reveal action of RPS is designed to be unpredictable, forever. So, in this sense, it makes sense to consider simultaneous reveal "random," even though it technically isn't actually random. Actually—if you want to get really technical— even dice rolls and card draws aren't actually random, they're responding to the laws of physics in a deterministic way. But since we can never predict those things, by design, we call them "random."

This would be in contrast to a deterministic gameplay mechanism that can, slowly but surely, get solved.

Maybe you'll dominate an enemy force twice your size. Maybe you'll get destroyed by a force half your size, or anything in between.

Regardless of what happens, after that point the entire game-state is now being informed by that sudden injection of noise. In Risk, of course, the game is constantly getting these noise-injections throughout the game.

So while there is certainly some skill to the game of Risk, it takes many, many plays to actually see it. If an unskilled player were to play a skilled player five times, it's not inconceivable that the unskilled player could win all five of those games.

At best, what we have is an incredibly inefficient game. Most games that utilize high output randomness aren't very interesting to begin with, and use output randomness's gambling-values ("I hope I roll a six!") to maintain any interest. However, if you were to introduce this kind of randomness into an interesting system, it would be very frustrating. Players would be excited about exploring the possibility space, but having some random event shut them down while they're trying to do that is the game simply getting in their way. Basically, they have to keep playing until all or most of the random outcomes happen the way they "should"—the way they're most likely to. Then, and only then, can they start to get a somewhat clear picture in terms of feedback for their play.

To make things worse, high levels of output randomness simply make a game unfair. At the start of a match, both players should have—as far as the system is concerned—an equal chance to win. The only determining factor should be "the quality of the decision-making." However, the series of dice rolls and card draws will almost always favor one player over another, if even only by a small amount, and that's not good. That's especially a problem when two players are very closely matched, in which case it might be randomness deciding the games.

Human beings are very good at attaching agency to random events, which is why we see animals in the clouds and fictional characters on our breakfast toast. In the same way, when we get a win in a game, we're pretty good at attributing it to our own performance. This might seem like a "win–win"—the losers feel like it wasn't their fault that they lost, and the winners feel like it was their fault that they won. But ultimately, both of these are deceptive and illusory, and it's counterproductive to build a contest of decision-making in this way. Again: you don't want your system to have legs because it's deceiving the player; you want it to be interesting to the player.

With highly random games, it's simply very difficult to tell when exactly you won because the randomness favored you, or if you won because of your great decision-making. Good games don't need this kind of noise slowing players down on their quest to climb the mountain of understanding your game.

High randomness is the mark of a game that is insecure with its degree of depth; it's the equivalent of a new visual artist's overuse of smudging or a new guitar player's overuse of distortion.

UNFAIR INPUT RANDOMNESS

It's not just output randomness that can interject an unfair bit of noise that artificially delays the point where a player could have gained some understanding. Input randomness, when it varies in "difficulty" for the player (i.e., some games things are arranged in a way that's advantageous to the player, sometimes disadvantageous), can have a similar effect on games as output randomness. In both cases, players need to play many games to get reliable feedback on their play.

Unlockables/Asymmetry

Another way to deceive players is to break up the game into smaller parts and only allow the player to see a small portion of the game at a time. For example, if a game starts you off with one set of rules, but there are new gameplay modes or levels that can be unlocked, that fact is always there in the back of your mind as you're playing. So even if you're not having a great time, there's always this "other" thing that the game also has.

Videogame-style asymmetry, where you choose a character or faction before the game begins, also can have this effect. There's a "grass is greener" feeling, where, whatever character you chose, while you're playing you imagine the others as being probably more interesting. This illusion can keep players playing for far longer than if there was just the one character.

Visual Immersion

A very common practice in videogames is to make your game visually immersive—that is to say, to visually portray the game's elements in such a way that makes the player, to some extent, feel like they're "really there." The most obvious way this is employed is via a first-person point-of-view camera, as seen in titles like *Counter-Strike* or *Elder Scrolls V: Skyrim*. In these titles—especially in the highly fantasy-simulation-dependent *Skyrim*—part of the idea is to "immerse" the player in the world.

The problem is, this isn't where "immersion" really comes from. Ever notice how people get incredibly immersed in a great novel? What could be further away from the literal, realistic portrayal of reality that *Skyrim* brings than a set of glyphs in black and white printed on dead trees? And yet novels routinely engage people to the point where they are completely and utterly immersed.

The myth is that immersion comes from visual/auditory messages, but the problem is the human mind wanders quickly. We're curious and inquisitive and while a picture-perfect image might in fact immerse us for a moment, if there isn't an engaging system there for us to keep us immersed, we'll quickly snap out of it and remember that we're just tinkering with some computer program.

The thing that engages people in interactive systems is actually quality interaction—for games, this means interesting, difficult and meaningful decisions as frequently as possible.

One might ask, "well, then shouldn't the answer be to make an interesting system that *also* visually immerses?" Perhaps "*Minecraft* with better graphics in a VR headset" would be one concept. The answer to that is that actually, again, the visuals really lose their value once interactive engagement comes into play. So, while visual immersion might be useful for "getting people in the door," its utility quickly drops off after that point.

DECEIVING THE DESIGNER

There are two types of "deception" that can happen with regards to game design. The first type is "deceiving the player," as we just discussed.

But the other type is the designer deceiving himself. Of course, all of the things that deceive a player can deceive a designer. High output randomness can make a designer think that his system has more to it than it does, just as it would for a player.

There are also qualities, however, that tend to affect the designer more as he's designing the game. They can, and do, affect players, but they are qualities that a designer should be especially on the lookout for.

Mass Content/Complexity

Having a large amount of content in a game can make it seem like it works better than it actually does, especially if there's a huge amount of content that comes into play in a single game. For example, if you have a card game and there are 150 different types of cards in play, it might seem like the game is exciting and dynamic (assuming  you've done some basic balancing work on them). Players will make crazy combinations, come back from certain death, and more—in general, the system will surprise players.

However, this is really only because the players haven't played enough to memorize all of those rules, not because the system itself is actually deep. Further, having a huge amount of content draws the designer's attention away from improving the system and towards improving these many little bits of content.

Mass content also tends to be restrictive in how deep your system can even be in the first place. The larger the amount of content that must be usable in the system, the less deep the system itself can be. A great example is the famous collectible card game Magic: The Gathering. The game has thousands upon thousands of cards, which means the system has to be almost nothing to support that. It can't be anything like a clockwork system; it can't be a tight web of interconnected mechanisms. The best it can really hope to be is a big box which you fill up with stuff, shake around, and dump out on the floor.

Somewhat related is the fact that content-heavy games are impossible to balance. This is because, ultimately, there is only a small number of "true roles" in your game. As a hypothetical example, let's say there are 200 characters in your game: a third of them are wizards, a third are fighters, and a third of them are priests. The game requires you to use at least one of each of these. Ultimately, players are simply going to hone in on whichever of the wizards is the best wizard, and use him. Even if it's some tiny, almost indescribably small difference between Wizard X and Wizard Y, one of them is going to be slightly better for the job.

Producing all that content also costs a lot. Now, if it were what good game design called for, then no cost is too high, but it isn't. Think of all the many hundreds of man-hours wasted building those hundreds of spells— and, ultimately, just a small fraction of it actually ends up being relevant.

Novelty

If we see someone dancing poorly, we might walk away unimpressed. But if we see a bear dancing poorly, the very same dance moves might be highly impressive all of a sudden, mostly because of the novelty of it. This is what's known as the "dancing bear"  phenomenon. Translated to games, this usually means that the designer is starting out with some premise or technological platform that essentially reduces the expectations of the potential viewer. Examples would be a game that runs on a watch or that only uses sound.

The difference between a gimmick and a non-gimmick technological advancement is that a gimmick typically reduces our expectation but increases the novelty, whereas a legitimate technological advancement increases our expectation.

Less common examples of gimmicks or novelty might also include so-called "art games"—applications that have some kind of mechanical game-like functionality, but are also trying to make some kind of statement unrelated to gameplay, such as "I love my father" or "loneliness causes psychological damage," for example. At the time of this writing, such things are novel, and they also greatly reduce the expectation from players in this regard. There may be incredibly flat, boring gameplay, but any attempt to point this out might be met with a statement like, "but it's an art game."

There is technological novelty, which we get every few years in the form of new gaming consoles such as the next PlayStation or Xbox console. If you rebuild a game, make it 90% the same as the game you made last year, but put it on the new hardware, that could seem like enough of a reason for the new version to exist. This is an extremely common type of deception.

This is precisely the problem with working with gimmicks or novelty—they give you, the designer, an excuse to not be harsh on your own work.

Genre

Working with a genre in mind while designing a game can be a problem. One issue is similar to novelty, in that it gives us excuses for our mistakes. "Why does this RTS have map scrolling? It's terrible  that I have to slide my mouse around on the screen to fix the camera." Answer: that's what you do in an RTS. Designers won't usually consciously think that, but they will certainly allow themselves to be boxed in by design standards of their genre, and, when challenged, they might sort of just shrug it off without knowing why.

Further, many "genres," especially in digital games, are actually complete game designs. The "2D fighter," for instance, already carries with it 90% of a designer's job: it already has "actors in a rectangle," "health bars," "attacks that deal damage to health," "blocking," "throwing that counters blocking," etc. All the "designer" has to do is add his characters

GAME DESIGNERS AND GENRE

At the time of writing, the role of the game designer is often overlooked, and sometimes even dismissed as being unimportant. A frequent criticism of designers is that they are "idea guys." Given that so many game designers operate within a genre, and that most genres are actually complete game designs, this criticism is often actually reasonable! Ultimately, however, those people working inside complete-game-genres really aren't designers—they really are idea guys. The digital games world still needs to really be introduced to the power of good game design.

and special moves—and perhaps a new rule, like a new Super Move bar, or something—and he's done.

So, while genre can be helpful at the very inception of a game, it quickly loses its utility and becomes a burden for designers.

Toy

Some games have a "toy-like" quality to them. These games may be imbalanced or shallow, but as long as they have enough complexity to allow players to try weird things, players—and the designer—might be deceived.

A common example of this is games that include a physics system of some kind. Especially if it does something somewhat new with physics, such as combine character animation with physics, it can be quite spectacular to see what happens when you do this or that to a model.

For a designer who's not acutely aware of the difference between toys and games, it's impossible to tell the difference between "toy-fun" and "game-fun." In the case of toy-fun, players are making suboptimal moves for the sake of entertaining themselves (sometimes, this is referred to as "style points"). For example, in the card game Dominion players often go for suboptimal, high-risk strategies just to "see if it's possible" to get some insane amount of points, or to fill the other players' decks with curses, or to buy up all of the Duchy cards, etc.

Having a system that is prone to "toy-fun" is dangerous, because it draws the designer to want to add more "toy-like" elements—things that snowball out of control, or have crazy effects.

Often, the addition of such crazy effects throws the idea of balance—or even strategy in general—completely out the window.

Story/"Moral Choices"

Some designers are eager to add narrative elements to their games. A common route is to have some sort of text pop up at a certain point laying out some story details. The single-player game *FTL* has popups that appear from time to time detailing a story about, say, a guy who's been  stranded on a space platform for many years. You have the option of taking him on board and rescuing him or leaving him there to die.

On its face, this seems like an interesting choice, particularly because there's a bit of a "moral" element to it that colors it. However, it's really not an interesting choice at all. We'll discuss the moral element in a moment, but remove that from the equation for now. If you take him on the ship, there is some chance it will do something good, and some chance it will do something bad. Sometimes he'll give you some high value trinket that he had with him. Sometimes he'll go crazy and kill one of your crewmembers. Not taking him on usually just means nothing happens. So basically, the game is just asking you:

Do you want to flip a coin? Heads = something good happens, tails = something bad happens.

This is not an interesting choice to make. Also, if it's not random, then there is just some correct answer that must be memorized. Dressing up this flat, random choice with narrative elements does not change how flat and uninteresting it actually is.

Another thing that has been argued is that it's possible to implement a "moral" dimension into a game. The way that this would manifest would perhaps be something like the following choice: you must choose to either save the man and get one point or grab the golden trinket and gain five points. In this situation, it's argued, players face a "moral dilemma," where it's difficult to make the choice—and not because it's a difficult choice in terms of strategy, but because we are deciding whether a person will live or die.

There are major problems with this thinking. First of all, understand that morality in the real world is simply a set of rules that we employ to reach a goal—almost always something like "making the world a better place" (we can disagree somewhat on what that means exactly, of course). Games, however, have their own sets of rules and their own goals. Players understand when they're playing a game that they are in fact *playing a game* and they are playing by the game's rules. If "morality" were really something that could challenge a game's actual rules and goals, then how would people be able to play something like a modern war game, where both sides are human beings of different countries? You're shooting a person in the face, a person who has a family and friends, just like you do. Does that cause people—even highly moral people—even a moment of doubt about whether they should do it? Of course not. We understand that while we're playing a game, we're playing by *its* rules, not by the rules of the greater world that we live in.

Section 2 **MY EXPERIENCES**

While I have worked on dozens of projects over the years, there are three projects that I've worked on that really paint a clear picture for why the clockwork design pattern is necessary. Those three games are *100 Rogues*, an iOS *Rogue*-like dungeon-crawler; *Empire: The Deck-Building Strategy Game* (a 4X-strategy/deck-building tactical war-game); and *Auro: A Monster-Bumping Adventure* (a hex-based dungeon-crawler). Each of these games, and the experience of working on them, serves as at least anecdotal validation of the clockwork game design theory.

100 ROGUES—A TYPICAL DESIGN PROCESS

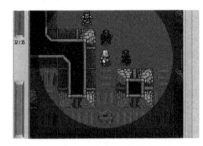

100 Rogues. Copyright Fusion Reactions

When I started designing *100 Rogues* in late 2008, I was basically approaching the problem the same way that most people do for their first few commercial games. I started with a genre, and then basically just added things that "seemed like they would be cool." There was no formal process or philosophy behind the actions, but rather just a long series of from-the-hip guesses.

This wasn't because I didn't care to know about how to design games well. I prided myself at the time as being a strong game designer. I had read most of the big, well-known game design books, I had my own design blog, and I had been designing games most of my life. It was because, despite having all this exposure, I still had never been exposed to any real, constructive answers for how to design games.

100 Rogues is essentially a *Rogue*-like game—a term used to describe "games that are like the 1980 computer game *Rogue*." You have a single avatar, and you traverse procedurally generated dungeons, collecting treasure, leveling up RPG-style, and gaining points. Both *100 Rogues* and *Rogue* have a similar unclear goal, in that they have a numeric score (which suggests a point-based goal), but they also have a completion state (you can "beat the game").

The game wasn't terribly difficult to design, but only because I was rather unaware of a lot of the problems that my design decisions were introducing. Also, much of my design work was very ineffective due to the lack of a strong core system.

For example, I had the idea of introducing more "tactical spells" to the genre—spells that affect a certain area, that move or displace actors, or that do "utility" functions such as blind opponents. All of these involved using the game's grid in a way that would maximize its utility. I understood at this point that it would be smart to really *use* that grid for something, and so my answer was to sort of slap "tactical abilities" onto the existing *Rogue* structure.

This wasn't totally ineffective, of course. There are some moments when you actually do use your abilities in interesting ways. The problem is that the game simply wasn't built to support these moments, so they were few and far between.

I mentioned the fact that high levels of unfair randomness in your design can actually obstruct your ability to design. With *100 Rogues*, this happened to me, in an interesting way. The problem was, ironically, that the randomness of the game actually made it too easy to design and balance. When there's excessive randomness everywhere, everything is cloudy, and every ability you design "basically works." This is how systems like RPGs have so much content. So while I didn't have a ton of trouble designing the abilities for the game, the fact is that I should have. There were problems existing that I just couldn't see.

The fact is that *100 Rogues*—like most videogames—doesn't *have* a core mechanism. From where it is, there are a few directions it could go in terms of finding a core, but in any case, you'd almost certainly be left with something that's unrecognizable from what it is now. Probably the thing that is the biggest draw of *100 Rogues* and all *Rogue*-lookalikes is actually the randomness itself: these systems are inherently closest to gambling machines like Slots or Pachinko. They are built largely on the illusion of choice.

Ironically, at the time I was already a little bit sensitive to unfair/ output randomness, so I actually took a lot of steps to minimize the random effects. At the same time, the system didn't have a strong core, so it couldn't be a strong strategy game either. So, currently, it sort of hovers in a no-man's-land, with unclear goals, no strong system, and is not even really random enough to be a good gambling machine. Players are forced to apply a lot of effort on their own part to "play designer" and make it fun in their own ways, by creating their own little challenges for themselves. In this way—again, like many videogames—*100 Rogues* is highly inefficient.

Further, development itself was very difficult. Have you heard the expression "feature creep" or "mission creep?" Both refer to the propensity for a project to grow and grow and grow. People get new ideas, they seem good or even great, and in they go, even if they weren't originally planned. Of course, you can get around some of this by having a tight schedule, but, at the same time, you never want to let a schedule stop you from making your game great if you have the opportunity. A good schedule should plan for some leeway in this regard.

Throwing Items

In *100 Rogues*, there are items: equippable items, consumable items, and so on. In many *Rogue*-like games, including *Mystery Dungeon: Shiren the Wanderer* and *Dungeon Crawl: Stone Soup* (both of which I was playing a lot at the time), you can literally throw any item, and they become a damaging projectile that you can attack monsters with. Some items have interesting properties when thrown.

Other games that were similar had this feature, and somewhat late in development, I got it in my head that this feature was so great it really just had to be in the game. We delayed things a bit and crunched extra hard to get the feature in by launch. It was very difficult and we had a much rockier release because of it.

And was the feature really needed? Who knows. That's the problem with a patchwork design—you have no way of answering the question of what really is or is not needed. Normally, we'd ask, "well, are 'throwing items' a necessary supporting mechanism, needed to support the core mechanism?" But that was not possible in *100 Rogues*, and some damage was caused to the game because of this fact.

EMPIRE—INTERESTING MECHANICS AREN'T ENOUGH

Although *Empire: The Deck-Building Strategy Game* was released in 2013, I actually designed the basics of it years prior. In 2012 I was approached by a team that wanted to make a "4X strategy game," and they liked the design, so I went for it. For whatever reason, even though I had just finished writing my first book on the topic, I failed to see the critical design flaw in *Empire*: it had no core mechanism.

In the game, there are two main "screens" where gameplay takes place. This already should have been a warning to me, as quite often when a game has more than one gameplay screen this often means that you have two large mechanisms that are fighting with each other. In one screen—the

Empire. Copyright Crazy Monkey Studios

overmap—you would build and improve cities, launch attacks, manage an army, etc. In the other screen, you would do battle.

Both of these gameplay screens have a lot of really interesting gameplay mechanisms. For instance, on the overmap your city actually drains the resources from surrounding tiles, meaning that, eventually, cities are costing you more than they're gaining you, and you are forced to eventually abandon cities and move on. This means that the old *Civilization* trope of these massive dinosaur cities that live forever was no longer an issue. It also had a way of moving gameplay along and keeping things dynamic and transient. Players had to make hard choices about when to abandon, especially since abandonment also increased the threat level of nearby monsters.

The battle screens also were quite interesting, taken on their own. The game involved a small grid, with two armies facing one another. Each turn you have a chance to play an ability, and then all of your units move one tile forward, and any units that can attack, do. So, it's a bit like an automated, randomized chess, that you can throw moves into to sway the battle one way or the other.

I had generally advanced a lot as a designer and so I was able to avoid many game design pitfalls. However, I didn't avoid the fundamental pitfall of "having no core mechanism." Both "screens" were almost a complete game in and of themselves; they fought each other constantly, and beyond a complete rehaul from near-scratch (which there weren't the resources for post-release, understandably), it was not fixable. All I could do was brute-force cram square pegs into round holes so that they sort of fit, for a while.

That is the lesson of *Empire*: strategy games need a core mechanism. Even if you do everything else right, no core mechanism means eternal problems. It's a nice, beautiful and sturdy castle, built on a swamp.

Auro

AURO—A CORE MECHANISM GAME

The last game of the three I will bring up in this section is *Auro: A Monster-Bumping Adventure*. While one way that *100 Rogues* could have been improved was to turn it into a straight-up gambling machine, in many ways, *Auro* is what would happen if you took it in the opposite direction.

When I first started designing *Auro*, I actually—again—started with the *Rogue*-like genre. My initial idea was to "boil down" the *Rogue*-like into something super-efficient, where almost every input was an interesting decision. I began by "boiling off" feature after feature that seemed like chaff. No more XP and RPG-style leveling up/stats. No more random-to-hit dice rolls. No more "inventory" and "items." Instead of huge sprawling non-linear levels, short, linear, and tight levels.

To my horror, I found that when you boiled off all of the chaff from *Rogue*, you were left with nothing. *Auro*, in its early iterations, was literally just an actor moving around on a grid, tapping monsters to kill them. They died in one shot, since there was no health system, and there was no chance of missing. So the game was solved, unexciting, and flat.

For a while, I experimented with some random things, trying to figure out how to make this nothing into a something. We tried all kinds of abilities out, looking for an idea—it was basically a big digital scratchpad for strategy game design.

At one point, we had an ability called "trap," which allowed you to drop a trap in place next to you. If a monster walked onto the trap, he would bounce two tiles in the direction he was moving. There was a question about what happened if the monster hit a wall during his flight, and I came up with the crazy idea that maybe the walls weren't walls—maybe, instead, the floor was surrounded by water, and when monsters flew off of the side, they splashed into the water and were killed.

Soon after, I realized that this would be an excellent core mechanism. It's not too direct: you can't just tap on monsters to kill them. It's context-sensitive: there needs to be water in the direction you knock the monster in order to kill them. It's expandable: spells could create things that modified tiles that helped you knock monsters out, or that changed the way that monsters moved.

Floe

Auro took a long time to design, but the process was smooth and constantly improved. Having the core mechanism in place—which we referred to as "bumping"—allowed us to constantly have something to check all of our work against. Does this new ability support making bumping interesting? Or does it step on the toes of bumping?

One ability we designed early on and that stuck around until release was "floe." Floe allowed you to create an area of slippery ice tiles.

Monsters, when bumped on the ice, would slide all the way to the end of the ice. Floe also has many other uses—for instance, you can cast it out over water to walk on water and create new pathways around obstacles, or you can lure heavy monsters onto it, who crash through and drown.

Since the game is all about bumping, it makes sense to have an ability that changes what happens when a monster is bumped back. Since positioning is also a major supporting mechanism, it's great that floe allows you to maneuver over water, creating new angles of approach.

On the other hand, we had another ability called "ice wall." Ice wall created big, heavy bricks of ice that blocked off areas, quite like the pillars that would appear in the rest of the game. We tried *so* many things to make ice walls work.

- We tried making them bricks that you spawn, and then you can bump those bricks around, creating floe in the process.
- We tried making them only appear as a result of freezing a monster. That monster would be taken out of play, but you could never kill them, which seemed interesting.
- We tried giving them a neat "on/off" relationship with floe, where you hit one ability and it turns all floe into ice bricks and all ice bricks into floe. Seemed really interesting!

Ultimately, however, ice wall was inherently fighting against the core mechanism of bumping. It created obstacles that jammed up the play field making it harder to bump things. Eventually we realized this and the entire ability was scrapped. Without a core mechanism to compare it against, it might have taken us longer to figure out the problem—or we might have never found it at all.

When a game has a core mechanism, as *Auro* does, it almost designs itself. You're fighting *with* the forces of logic, instead of against them, in a way.

Section 3 **CLOSING THOUGHTS**

This concludes the explanation of the clockwork game design pattern. My hope is that for those who do utilize it in their designs, they can work smarter and end up with a vastly better result. Even for those who don't utilize it, hopefully it will get people thinking along a more constructive path than the one we have been on.

It may feel strange or dogmatic for many to think that there could be such a clear, black-and-white guideline for strong game design as this book suggests. We've developed a culture that distrusts easy answers, and, for the most part, this distrust is helpful and wise.

The thing is, some answers really *are* easy, and we're much better off knowing them than not knowing them. The equation for finding the radius of a circle. The rule of thirds in visual composition. A central thesis for essay-writing. These are patterns that we have discovered, and our craft has made leaps and bounds because of their discovery.

Further, having these tools does not make our *job* easy. Instead, it makes our work effective. It means that every hour we spend working gets us further and, since we live in a finite universe, that means that we end up with straight-up better games.

I have no doubt that, if not this book, then books like this book will be a crucial part of developing our discipline from its current primitive state into a mature and sophisticated craft. Those who are reading this book around the time of its writing are lucky in that they will likely witness this transition during their lifetime. The more focused you are on finding concrete answers to difficult questions, the more likely that becomes.

So, thank you for reading, and thank you for participating.

INDEX